This book is lovingly dedicated to the Presbyterian women in my family, spanning three generations: Alma Fields Reinhard, Tressa Reinhard Jones, Elizabeth Reinhard Sheppard, and especially my mother, Ann Jones Catron.

Contents

Introduction

The concept for this book began as a series of Bible studies prepared for the 2003 Gathering of Presbyterian Women.[1] The theme of the conference, "God's Vision, Our Calling," grew out of the planning committee's prayerful consideration of Ephesians 4:1–6, the Scripture passage for the event:

> I therefore, the prisoner in the Lord, beg you to lead a life worthy of the calling to which you have been called, with all humility and gentleness, with patience, bearing with one another in love, making every effort to maintain the unity of the Spirit in the bond of peace. There is one body and one Spirit, just as you were called to the one hope of your calling, one Lord, one faith, one baptism, one God and Father of all, who is above all and through all and in all.

Working with this Scripture as a base, I began to look at other biblical passages that address the dual theme of God's grand design and our Christian calling. As one might expect, I found numerous connections to the Ephesians text and its themes in both Old and New Testament writings. Moreover, six subthemes related to the larger theme of our calling kept repeatedly coming to the fore. Together with the theme of God's vision, these have formed the outline for this book.

From start to finish, the Bible indicates that there is an intimate connection between God's long-term vision and our immediate calling. The core of this can be seen in the Bible's own construction, in which the vast majority of Scripture describes the human struggle of real life as it falls between the goodness of the original creation (Genesis) and the future glory of the realm of God (Revelation). Time and again, the message of the biblical writers comes down to this: God has a vision of wholeness for us and for the world that the first creation modeled and that the new creation will bring to permanent fruition; in the meantime, God calls us to create as much of that wholeness as we can on earth right now. The Ephesians passage taps into this overarching divine vision by centering on wholeness within the community of faith. Only when we live in unity in the Spirit, the passage suggests, are we able to fulfill our calling and usher in a bit of God's realm into the here and now.

This book looks at six aspects of our calling as Christians and how this calling relates to God's own vision. We will begin in the first chapter with a look at what the Bible tells us about God's grand plan. Chapters 2 and 3 will then explore the covenant relationship that God establishes with us and the role our choice plays in

---

This book is a thematic study of the topic "God's Vision, Our Calling." Each of the seven chapters focuses on a single subtheme related to the overall study, often drawing on a variety of biblical texts for insights. Each chapter also includes extra information in sidebars, as well as questions for reflection at the end.

As further aids to the reader, the book contains a pronunciation guide for Greek and Hebrew words and a short list of suggested readings for further study. Two appendixes provide additional Bible background for more complicated texts referenced in the study itself.

developing that relationship to its fullest. Chapters 4 and 5 focus on the new identity that we gain through the covenant and on our subsequent response in a new way of life. Finally, chapters 6 and 7 discuss the gifts with which God has made us competent for service and the role of ministry to which we are all called.

"God's Vision, Our Calling"—it's a timely theme. Certainly, recapturing God's vision for the world, the church, and ourselves is vitally important for Christians today. The good news is that not only is this possible, it's a promise. As we seek to "lead a life worthy of the calling to which [we] have been called" (Eph. 4:1), we become the conduit through which God will transform all these areas—the world, the church, and even ourselves—according to the ever-gracious divine vision.

1

An Overarching Plan

One of the marks of being Christian is seeking God's direction, being open to God's voice, and following God's will. Accordingly, one of the great questions for Christians through the ages has been, "What does God want of me and of the church?" We have been blessed with two key sources of inspiration and guidance when it comes to seeking an answer: the Bible and the voices of others in the faith community.

The Bible, of course, is the primary means we have of knowing God and the history of God's loving acts throughout time. It gives us insight into the nature of God and the vision that God has for us, the church, and the world. Moreover, taken as a whole, the Bible provides a lens through which we can test *our own* vision to ensure that it aligns with God's.

> ## Ephesians 1:8–10
>
> "With all wisdom and insight he has made known to us the mystery of his will, according to his good pleasure that he set forth in Christ, as a plan for the fullness of time, to gather up all things in him, things in heaven and things on earth."

The image of the Bible as a lens has become particularly meaningful to me in light of a gift I received a few years ago from a Presbyterian woman. This dear friend, a pastor in Texas, presented me with a unique cross made of ammunition shell casings. Both shells were capped at each end, so the four corners of the cross appear to be covered in brass stubs. In reality, the horizontal shell holds a lovely surprise. Filled with bits of mica and broken glass behind glass on one end, and equipped with an eyepiece on the other, it is a small (but quite workable) kaleidoscope. In handing me the cross, my friend said, "I like this because it reminds me of the way the world works. All the broken bits and pieces, all the chaos and meaningless slivers, take on a beautiful pattern when you look at it through the cross of Jesus Christ. I hope this cross reminds you to view the world through God's eyes, and not your own."

> Ephesians begins with a bold statement: God has been working out a divine plan in secret, which has now been revealed to us. While the letter goes on to speak about that plan specifically in terms of *reconciliation*, its concern for how Christians recognize and respond to God's intentions is a microcosm of what we find in the Bible itself.

Unlike the kaleidoscope, however, which always shows a shifting pattern, the Bible helps us to see the overall, constant goal of God. From beginning to end, the Bible affirms that God has a plan and that God's intent to enact that plan has never wavered. God has a vision, and we have been invited to share in it.

To understand this vision, one really does have to look from one end of the Bible to the other—indeed, from one end of time to the other. By looking at what God intended at the start and at what God promises will come in the end, we find critical clues to God's overarching plan.

IN THE BEGINNING

"In the beginning . . . God created the heavens and the earth." Genesis 1:1 and the subsequent story of creation (Gen. 1:2–2:4a) encapsulate God's original intent for the world. When we add the next passage, which is a more intimate version of the creation of human beings (Gen. 2:4b–25), we see four things about God's plan at the start.

First, the purpose of creation is life. It is somewhat easy to miss this point if we focus solely on the glories of the universe, including the infinite expanse of distant stars and galaxies. The creation accounts in Genesis 1–2 make it clear, however, that the ultimate goal of God's creation is life—particularly human life. The universe, in all its mysterious complexity, exists to give us a place to be.

One strand of thought that runs throughout the Hebrew Bible makes this particularly clear. This interpretation of creation does not maintain that God created the universe out of nothing; rather, this view understands the "formless void" of Genesis 1:1 to refer to the raw matter of chaos, a dangerously destructive substance.[1] In this Hebrew understanding, God did not take the raw chaos and convert it into the elements of creation. Instead, God pushed back this destructive force and cleared a place in which the universe could exist. In the traces of this view that run through the Old Testament, we see a frightened awareness that the chaos is always out there—always ready to rush in and destroy—and a heartfelt gratitude that God continues to choose to hold the chaos at bay. Indeed, the overall affirmation is that God will *always* choose to protect us and the rest of creation from such obliteration, because that is the nature of God. God is the One who always chooses life over death, creation over destruction.

Second, God intended life to be good. The creation accounts in Genesis revel in the life that God produces, and they highlight

God's delight in every detail. Step by step, God created all that is, and, at the end of each stage, God saw the results as "good." When at last human beings were created and God was finished, God looked at everything that had been made and "indeed, it was very good" (Gen. 1:31). From the beginning, God's created world was most excellently made, and every aspect of creation had value in God's eyes.

To underscore the value of living entities, the text assures us that part of God's initial plan was that all plants and animals, human beings included, would have everything they needed. All the elements for survival have been carefully crafted into creation. What's more, God not only provided the basics of food and shelter for all living beings in sufficiency, God provided these things in abundance. God did not merely intend created beings to have enough, God intended them to have that and more.

Third, God intended life to be whole. Genesis makes clear that, when it comes to human beings, God's original plan included more than an abundance of food and shelter. God also intended people to have meaningful relationships and spiritual fulfillment. Together, the two accounts of creation in Genesis 1–2 picture a world in which people lack for nothing on the physical, intellectual, emotional, and spiritual levels. Moreover, according to God's original plan, human society is designed to reflect this same wholeness throughout every level: from the individual to the family to the local community to the nation to the world at large. Granted, one has to reach beyond the first two chapters of Genesis to see this spelled out clearly, but the Bible does affirm such far-reaching wholeness as part of God's overall intent for human beings.

One hint of this divine desire lies in Genesis 2:25, in which the man and woman are described as "not ashamed." Modern Christians tend to connect this section of the verse with what immediately precedes it—the fact that the man and woman were naked—and limit its significance to one of three meanings: (1) that the man and woman had a natural innocence at this stage, like children, which made them unself-conscious; (2) that sex as originally intended by God was natural and completely comfortable, both physically and emotionally; or (3) both of the above. In fact, the concept of shame runs throughout the Old Testament as a measure of broken covenants. In the Genesis account, the lack of shame means far more than an ease with nudity or sexuality; it is a state of being that comes from unbroken, right relationships with God and one another. Other scriptural passages, especially from the Prophets in the Old Testament and the Gospels and Epistles in the New Testament, make it very clear that such wholeness is what God has always intended for humanity at every level of society.

Fourth, God intended us to be responsible partners. The wholeness God intends does not stop at the limits of human society, however. It is for the entire creation. In God's initial plan, every interaction of human beings—whether with one another or with nature—is intended to nurture and promote the life and goodness that God gave at the start. Indeed, the suggestion of military language in Genesis 2:15 makes this startlingly apparent: here, God places the first human being in the midst of the created world in order to *garrison* or *defend* it (most translations say "keep it"), in the same way that troops defend treasured property.

God has more than invited us to participate in maintaining the wholeness of creation; God has created us, in part, with this partnership in mind. In Genesis 1:28, God addresses men and women together and gives them "dominion" over all other living things. In this case, the language is not so much that of the military as that of a royal household. In the same way that earthly rulers appoint stewards to have oversight and care of their property, God's original plan cast human beings as the stewards of God's creation. From the beginning, God intended people to have care for the portions of creation they

The Vision from Genesis: Wholeness

Perhaps the Hebrew word that best encompasses the vision of God's original plan as represented in the creation accounts of Genesis is *shalom*. This word, often translated as "peace," means much more. It indicates the health, well-being, and prosperity both of individuals and of nations. In many prophetic writings it refers to conditions of economic and social justice for all members of the community. In some contexts it means "salvation." In the broadest sense of the word, though, *shalom* refers to the contented state of being that comes when relationships are whole and unbroken, whether these relationships are between members of a family, groups in society, or entire nations. *Shalom* most especially refers to the state of being that comes when *covenant* relationships are whole and unbroken—and that includes our relationship with God.

The Hebrew prophets connect the promise of eventual *shalom* to visions of the end time. Some passages hint at it by describing a return to Eden-like conditions (Isa. 11:1–9; Amos 9:13–15), while others overtly refer to conditions of *shalom* that will come under God's rule (Isa. 2:2–4; Mic. 4:1–4). For Christians, the most meaningful passages tend to be those that speak of a king to come who will initiate the age of *shalom* (Isa. 9:6; Mic. 5:2–5; Zech. 9:9–10).

could affect, and God envisioned people as responsible partners in that enterprise.

IN THE TIME TO COME

The vision of God's original plan for creation found in Genesis is intrinsically connected to the vision of the new heaven and new earth described in Revelation 21–22. There we see the final, irrevocable establishment of God's plan in full. In reading through these two chapters that close the Bible, we also see four elements of God's vision that echo and expand on the points from Genesis 1–2.

First, the purpose of the new creation is to bring God's original vision to fruition at last. The description of the new heaven and earth, and of the new Jerusalem in particular, shows that every aspect of God's original plan for creation will be implemented. God will reclaim the whole created order by making "all things new" (Rev. 21:5), thus restoring things as they should be. Note that in this process God does not eliminate or destroy the current creation, but transforms it.

Second, in the new creation life will be better than good. Having lived in a world that is less than perfect, we are in a position to appreciate fully the gifts that God offers in the new creation. Indeed, the text describes an existence where all of our physical, emotional, and spiritual needs will be met in abundance—and where all the negative aspects of current living will be missing. The writer especially emphasizes three things that will be "no more": the sea, which represents chaos and life-threatening danger (Rev. 21:1); death (v. 4a); and "mourning and crying and pain" (v. 4b). Everything that now robs life of its beauty and joy will be missing in God's perfect creation.

Third, in the new creation life will be complete. God's vision of *shalom* will finally be fulfilled on multiple levels. For instance, there will be peace and security on a social level, as indicated when Rev. 21:25 declares, "Its gates will never be shut by day—and there will be no night there." One of the reasons people gathered in cities behind closed gates was for safety and protection, and darkness was always a time to fear physical violence. In the time to come, however, all such threats will be removed, and the people will enjoy physical safety and peace.

> **Ephesians 6:23**
>
> "Peace be to the whole community, and love with faith, from God the Father and the Lord Jesus Christ."

There will also be peace and wholeness on a spiritual level. The entire new Jerusalem will function as a temple in which we have constant, direct access to God (21:22–23).[2] This perfect union with God, which represents a return to the state we

---

The Vision from Revelation: Completeness

Revelation speaks about a time when God's mystery, as stated in the King James Version, will be "finished" (10:7) and the words of God will be "fulfilled" (17:17). In both cases, the Greek word used is a form of the verb *teleo*, which is often translated as "to end" or "to bring to an end."

We misread the text, however, if we think of the action as stopping something in progress or eliminating something in existence. *Teleo* has a much more positive spin. It really indicates coming to rest because an ongoing process has been completed or fulfilled—much as God did on the seventh day of creation. Building on this root meaning, *teleo* was eventually associated with being perfect (lacking nothing). Among the other common translations for *teleo* are: to perform, to accomplish, and to finish. When applied to organic matter, *teleo* even came to mean "to mature."

When it comes to God's plan, *teleo* adds an important element in our understanding. It is the word Jesus used from the cross when he said, "It is finished" (John 19:30). The risen Christ uses a form of it again when he says, "I am the Alpha and the Omega, the first and the last, the beginning and the *end*" (Rev. 22:13; see 21:6; italics added). All things have been completed and fulfilled in Christ, including God's plan. The picture at the end of Revelation is not one of mass destruction but of wholeness and totality. Not one whit of God's original vision will be lost; rather, it will be complete at last.

---

had in Eden before the fall, is symbolized in part by our restored access to the tree of life (22:2; see also Gen. 2:9).

Best of all, this *shalom* will be for all peoples:

> In 21:3 John quotes Ezekiel 37:27, "My dwelling place shall be with them; and I will be their God, and they shall be my people," but the last word is modified to the plural, *"peoples"*. . . . The new Jerusalem is not populated by the "chosen people" only; the peoples of the earth, the very nations and even their kings (21:24!) that had opposed God's rule and oppressed the church, are here pictured as redeemed citizens of the Holy City.[3]

Fourth, in the new creation we will be more than partners with God. The vision of Revelation 21–22 shows that not only will we have eternal life, but we will reign with God over the new creation "forever and ever" (22:5). The effect of this co-rule that God grants will be cosmic, and life in the new Jerusalem will bring transformation to all the nations (21:24–26). Lest we forget our place and think we are equal to the Creator, however, the text also speaks of another activity besides reigning: We will spend eternity worshiping and serving God (22:3).

IN THE MEANTIME

The elements of God's vision that we see in Genesis and Revelation lead us to two unmistakable conclusions. First, we have a legitimate reason to hope. God intends goodness for us and for the world, and that goodness will win out. Second, we have an inescapable responsibility. We exist within God's plan and, accordingly, we are called to act in ways that embody it. As one writer puts it:

> John lets his picture speak for itself. His language throughout this vision is indicative: "This is how it will be." And yet as always the indicatives of biblical theology contain an implicit imperative, the gift becomes an assignment. If this is where the world, under the sovereign grace of God, is finally going, then every thought, move, deed in some other direction is out of step with reality and is finally wasted. The picture does not attempt to answer speculative questions about the future; it is offered as an orientation for life in the present.[4]

We may exist between the past time of God's original good creation and the future time of God's new creation, but in this "between time," God looks to us to create as much of the heavenly realm in the here and now as we can. This is the basis of, and the overall purpose for, our Christian calling. The rest of this book looks at six aspects of our calling in this light, beginning with our call to be in relationship with God and others as expressed through the notion of *covenant*.

◈◈◈◈◈

QUESTIONS FOR REFLECTION

1. What aspects of God's vision, as revealed in Genesis 1–2 and Revelation 21–22, most speak to you? Why? What other aspects of God's vision, if any, do you see beyond the ones listed in this chapter?

2. Where have you experienced new creation in your life? What still needs to be renewed within you? in your church?

3. What do you hope will be "no more" in God's realm? How might you and others speak and act accordingly in this age?

4. Are you hopeful about where life and creation is headed? Why? What evidence would your life provide to persuade others of that?

KEY LEARNINGS

- God has a grand master plan for creation.
- Genesis 1–2 shows that God's plan for creation from the beginning has been life and wholeness.
- Revelation 20–21 affirms that one day God will renew creation in the fulfillment of the divine plan.
- In the meantime, God invites us to be partners in this plan and expects us to act in ways that embody it.

2

Called to Relationship

Time and again, both the biblical texts and our own experience witness to the fact that we are created for relationship with other people and with God. The need to know others, interact with them, and be accepted by them runs so deeply in the human psyche that it directly affects our mental, emotional, and physical well-being. Moreover, there is growing scientific evidence that we are equally designed to yearn for a spiritual connection to something greater than ourselves.[1] The need for such relationships is, in essence, encoded in our gene pool.

The Bible interprets our need for connectedness as a call to relationship. As people of

> ## Ephesians 2:11–13
>
> "So then, remember that at one time you Gentiles by birth, called 'the uncircumcision' by those who are called 'the circumcision'—a physical circumcision made in the flesh by human hands—remember that you were at that time without Christ, being aliens from the commonwealth of Israel, and strangers to the covenants of promise, having no hope and without God in the world. But now in Christ Jesus you who once were far off have been brought near by the blood of Christ."

faith, we are not called to just any type of relationships, however, but to those that reflect God's overarching vision in some way. The biblical writers often describe such relationships in terms of *covenant*.

COVENANT IN THE OLD TESTAMENT

The Hebrew word for "covenant" is *berith*, which is not an easy word to translate into English. No one knows what the root of this word really is, but the best guess is that it comes from the Akkadian *beritu*, which means a bond or a binding. *Berith* indicates something that makes or forges a connection between two parties that is not to be broken. This is a voluntary binding, in that both parties agree to it willingly. In addition, this binding amounts to a new creation: *Berith* establishes a connection where there was not one before. In the Bible, this connection is both legal and sacred, even between two human parties.

Berith

Various versions of the Bible use different expressions to translate *berith*. In each case, the translators are doing their best to express one key meaning of the word out of several possibilities. So, for example, you may see:

- Agreement—used in the sense of two parties working together to find mutual understanding
- Contract—used in the sense of a legally binding agreement
- Testament—used in the sense of a "last will and testament"
- Promise—used to emphasize one's trustworthiness in following through on an agreement
- Vow—used to indicate an oath that is both legal and sacred
- Treaty—normally used to indicate an agreement between two formerly hostile groups
- Alliance—normally used to indicate an agreement between two formerly neutral groups
- Partnership—used to emphasize the equality and mutual responsibility of both parties

In the Old Testament, there are two primary types of covenant that we see: those that exist between humans, and those that exist between humans and God. The former instances of *berith* usually involve groups and are most often translated as "treaty," while the latter are most often translated as "covenant." Of course, both forms of covenant involve God at some level. In the human-to-human covenants, God is invoked as a witness and a guardian to ensure the agreement will be maintained. In the human-divine covenants, God is an active partner who always initiates the relationship.

There is a third type of *berith* as well, which is when God makes a covenant with nature or with animals. Perhaps the best example is the covenant God makes with creation after the flood (see Gen. 9). Although biblical scholarship generally considers most of these covenants with nature to be metaphorical, in the sense that nature itself cannot formally sign a contract, these incidents constitute a full covenant on an emotional and theological level. God makes promises, and God means them. At the same time, these covenants are different from the ones God makes with us, because they are one-sided: God makes promises to nature but asks nothing in return.

Covenants between Two Human Parties

In the Old Testament, covenants between two human parties take place in three ways:

1. as one human to another
2. as one group to another
3. as one nation to another

(See Appendix A for more detail on the three examples that follow.)

1. One Human in Relation to Another

In the whole Bible, there is only one example of a covenant that is made one on one between two humans: the covenant

made between David and Jonathan. First Samuel 18:1–4 out-
lines the heart of it: Because of the love these two friends bear
one another, they enter into a formal covenant relationship.[2]

When you find your best friend, often there is an eventual
impulse to do something to acknowledge and mark the significance of the relationship. That is part of what this scene is
about. At the same time, the covenant ceremony takes friendship to a new level. There is something absolutely sacred and
binding about the relationship Jonathan and David establish,
and we see this expressed in three elements:

1. The relationship is rooted in a special love similar to the
   love God shows us.
2. The relationship involves mutual responsibility and
   accountability on the part of both individuals.
3. God is present as witness to the relationship, both at the
   ceremony and from then on.

Let us consider first the type of love associated with this
covenant. There are different words for love in Hebrew, and
the one used here is special. It is not the normal word for the
love of friends or even family members. Rather, it is *hesed*—the
Hebrew word used almost exclusively to describe covenant
love. The Bible uses this word when it speaks of God's love as
being steadfast, faithful, and unfailing. It is love that is unconditional. It is love that sticks and doesn't end, regardless of
what the other does. It is love that waits and does not give up.
It is the love Paul describes in 1 Corinthians 13. In other
words, the love that Jonathan and David had for one another
is the kind of love that we are supposed to have for one another
as brothers and sisters in the Christian faith.

Out of their mutual love, Jonathan and David take an oath
to one another that solemnly establishes their mutual responsibility and accountability.[3] Each makes promises to the other
that amount to a guarantee always to put the other first and
seek the other's well-being at all costs. Jonathan and David

knew that love, no matter how deeply felt, has little meaning if it is not expressed in action. Thus they held themselves (and each other) accountable for acting in ways that bore visible witness to the love they had.

Finally, Jonathan and David called on God as a witness to their vows. Partly this was to add a level of seriousness to their commitment to one another that would not be there otherwise. Beyond that, however, Jonathan and David counted on God to help them continue to live out *hesed* love for one another in the days to come. Thus, in this example, as in all biblical covenants between two human parties, God was present at the ceremony and in all dealings afterward.

2. One Group in Relation to Another

A more common kind of covenant in the Old Testament takes place not between two individuals but between two clans or tribes. In such agreements, the groups were usually represented by the current chief or family head, whose word was binding for the others.

One example of this kind of covenant can be seen in the story of Jacob and Laban (Gen. 31:44–54). These two men were related by blood and by marriage—Laban was both Jacob's uncle and his father-in-law—but they each had good reason not to trust the other. A series of lies and tricks had led to severe tension between them. In the midst of a situation that threatened escalating violence, the men finally realized that their two households needed to come to some kind of agreement if they were to survive. So they sat down and began to iron out the details of a covenant agreement that would establish a cease-fire between them.

In verse 54, Jacob and Laban ratify their covenant treaty by eating a common meal together. The symbolism of this act is critical to understanding what the covenant accomplished. The treaty did more than just establish an uneasy peace between two disparate groups; it created a new legal and sacred status between these tribes, whereby they actually became as family should be. They moved from a state of constant threat to one that reflected bits of God's *shalom*.

These are the roots of the "family of God" imagery that carried forth into the early church. Indeed, this understanding of covenant as establishing peaceful family relationships where there were none before is part of God's vision that we live out in the meal we share at Christ's Table.

3. Nation to Nation

The third kind of human-to-human covenant that runs throughout the Old Testament is represented by the big political treaties that occurred between nations. In the ancient Near East, historical agreements of this type usually had six parts; many scholars see a similar structure in the Old Testament covenants with God. The six sections of such covenants are:

1. the preamble (or introduction) to the covenant
2. a prologue that tells the history of the two parties
3. the stipulations or rules of the covenant
4. provision for where the text will be kept and when the text will be brought out for a public reading to the people
5. a list of witnesses, including the deities of the respective nations
6. a list of blessings and curses contingent on whether one keeps the covenant.

On the political level of one nation dealing with another, the intent of a treaty was to create a relationship whereby the two groups of people would not fight one another but work together for mutual prosperity. Thus, again, the goal was *shalom*.

Covenants between Humans and God

At the heart of every covenant God originates with us is a single goal: "I will be your God, and you shall be my people" (Jer.

7:23; see also Exod. 6:7; Jer. 11:4; 30:22; Ezek. 36:28). This promise of an intimate and persistent bond can be found in the covenants with Abraham (Gen. 15 and 17), the people at Sinai (Exod. 19), David (2 Sam. 7), and the church (for example, see 1 Cor. 11:25; Heb. 8–9; 10:16).

In a world full of caprice, uncertainty, and animosity, God's covenants offer order, safety, and peace. After all, God has a purpose that we have already identified: to set us in a relationship of *shalom* with our Creator and with one another. God's covenants are all designed to help us achieve this end.

Following the pattern of historical treaties described earlier, the covenants with God tend to begin with a brief call to pay attention (the preamble), followed by a prologue that recounts what God has done with and for the people. This history is what gives human beings the courage and the faith to enter into partnership with God. The history reassures us as to who God is and how God operates. Because it grounds the covenant on what God has already done, we can trust the covenant promises made to us.

> ### Covenant and Election
>
> "The covenant is rightly understood in the context of election, God's choice of a people. Election is implicit throughout the history of Israel, but it is particularly emphatic in Deuteronomy and in Isaiah 40–55. One of the clearest statements of it is found in Deuteronomy 7:6–15, where it is evident that God elected Israel and entered into covenant strictly in the mystery of divine love. Moreover, God maintains the covenant in faithfulness and steadfast love. When the themes of election and covenant are examined throughout the Old Testament, it becomes clear that Israel was elected to privilege, obedience, and service as the covenant people." — Rhodes, 71

Next come the stipulations of the covenant. On the divine side, God promises to be steadfast and faithful in bringing the faith community into abundant blessings. Furthermore, God often indicates that these blessings will not be limited to the faith community alone, but will extend through it into the world. On the human side, the faith community is given laws to guide its way of relating to God and to others. In the traditional understanding of covenant, these laws are understood as an extension of God's love and grace; they are a type of "blueprint" by which God tries to show people how to begin building the heavenly realm on earth.

Like the ancient treaties, God's covenants can also stipulate where a text will be kept and when it will be read to the people. For example, shortly before his death Moses had the people renew their covenant with God. At that time he also wrote down the law (that is, the terms of the covenant) and instructed the priests to read it aloud every seven years in the presence of all the people (Deut. 31:10-13). The purpose of these public readings was twofold: (1) so that those who knew the covenant would not forget it but recommit to it, and (2) so that those who were unaware of the covenant or who had not heard its terms would have a chance to accept the blessings it offered.

Some of the covenants between God and people also include a list of witnesses. Of course, when God is one of the covenant partners, it's a little hard to call on God to be witness to that same treaty. So the list of witnesses on those occasions is usually drawn from the created order: mountains, hills, streams, and so on.[4] Moses even called on the *whole* created order to serve as a witness to the covenant renewal ceremony: "I call heaven and earth to witness against you today that I have set before you life and death, blessings and curses" (Deut. 30:19). After all, what better testament to God's faithfulness as a partner is there than the world God has already given us?

Finally, many of the divine covenants in the Bible include a detailed description of the blessings and curses that will follow, depending on whether the faith community keeps the covenant. These often emphasize the life that comes in keeping God's covenant and the death that comes outside of it (see, for example, Deut. 28).

THE "OLD" COVENANT AND THE "NEW"

When we move into the New Testament, there is a shift in the way covenant relationships are described. The Greek language did not have a word that was an exact equivalent of *berith*, so Greek-speaking writers used the closest parallel they could find in legal terminology: *diatheke*. This term originally referred to any legally binding arrangement of one's affairs, especially as it related to the disposition of one's property after death. In its most general secular usage, *diatheke* might be translated as "pact." Most often, however, it was used in the legal sense of "will" or "testament." That English translation for *diatheke* still lives on whenever we refer to either the Old or New "Testament" today.

Despite the difference in the Hebrew and Greek terms, however, the "old" and "new" covenants are more connected than one might think. God accomplished something unique in Christ, yet the Christ event is set fully in the context of God's prior relation with the world—and with the Hebrew people in particular. Thus Jesus was a Jewish man from a Jewish family, and he lived for the most part in a Jewish community. He grew up with Jewish Scripture, and he worshiped the Jewish God. He also placed himself squarely within the Old Testament concept of covenant, and he tried to teach the people what it truly meant.

In that sense, Jesus was in a long tradition of Jewish prophets who emphasized the covenant relationship as an attitude, not just external obedience to a set of laws. The core of their message was that the covenant relationship was to be in, of, and from the heart—and that one's actions then followed accordingly. Thus Moses spoke of a day when "the LORD your

God will circumcise your heart and the heart of your descendants, so that you will love the LORD your God with all your heart and with all your soul, in order that you may live" (Deut. 30:6). Jeremiah perhaps said it best when he prophesied:

> The days are surely coming, says the LORD, when I will make a new covenant with the house of Israel and the house of Judah. . . . [And] this is the covenant that I will make with the house of Israel after those days, says the LORD: I will put my law within them, and I will write it on their hearts; and I will be their God, and they shall be my people. No longer shall they teach one another, or say to each other, "Know the LORD," for they shall all know me, from the least of them to the greatest, says the LORD; for I will forgive their iniquity, and remember their sin no more. (Jer. 31:31, 33–34)

Jesus reclaimed this prophetic message and gave it concrete expression in his own person. Through his teachings, we get the sense that the former covenant is still in force, but now under far better terms. As Jesus said, "Do not think that I have come to abolish the law or the prophets; I have come not to abolish but to fulfill" (Matt. 5:17).

Moreover, his teachings often illustrated the *shalom* aspect of the covenant relationships to which we are called. The importance of an intact, loving relationship with God and others was so important, in fact, that when asked to cite the greatest commandment, Jesus replied: "'You shall love the Lord your God with all your heart, and with all your soul, and with all your mind.' This is the greatest and first commandment. And a second is like it: 'You shall love your neighbor as yourself.' On these two commandments hang all the law and the prophets" (Matt. 22:34–40; Mark 12:28–34; Luke 10:25–28).

The word for love Jesus used in these commandments is *agape*, the Greek equivalent to the steadfast covenant love (*hesed*) we discussed earlier. Whatever points theologians and Bible scholars may debate regarding how the "old" and "new" covenants relate to one another, one aspect is indisputable: *All* covenants with God are fulfilled through relationships that reflect the divine love God has for us.

God's love is best seen, of course, in Jesus' life, death, and resurrection—and in those momentous events God accomplished something that had never been achieved before. God in Christ broke down all the barriers that kept people from living fully into their covenant relationships, opening new ways to approach God and to relate to one another. Thus, Paul speaks of Jesus as a "mediator between God and humankind" (1 Tim. 2:5). The Greek word translated here as "mediator" is *mesites*, and it refers to a person who arbitrates between two parties to negotiate a pact or ratify a covenant. It can also refer to one who creates or restores harmony or friendship. Accordingly, the writer of the Letter to the Hebrews uses this same term to speak of Christ as one who has negotiated a covenant between us and God that is not only "new" (9:15; 12:24) but "better" (8:6).

THE NEW COVENANT IN CHRIST

When speaking of the new covenant we have in Christ, the New Testament writers often selected certain elements of Old Testament covenant theology and gave them new emphasis in light of the Christ event. Let's look at four of these aspects of the new covenant in Christ: remembrance, freedom, hospitality, and belonging.

1. *Remembrance.* This is a key concept in both testaments. After all, we can keep the covenant only insofar as we remember its terms and continue to honor them. What's more, part of our covenantal relationship with others involves remembering them—keeping them in mind, staying aware of them,

and lifting them up as a priority in our lives. This holds true for our relationship with God as well.

Forms of the verb *remember* run throughout many books of the Bible. For example, during the time of Israel's suffering as slaves in Egypt, God *remembered* the covenant with their ancestors and then brought about their deliverance. Throughout later generations, as the people of Israel celebrated the Passover event, they did so to *remember* what God did for them—to keep the original event fresh in people's minds so they could claim the story as their own. That is the same reason Jesus said at the Last Supper, "Do this in *remembrance* of me" (1 Cor. 11:24, italics added).

Just like the Passover event, the Lord's Supper is a remembrance that spans time. We remember a past event because it has direct implication for who we are and what we do today, but we are also anticipating a future event. The original Passover celebrated the fact that the people were literally on the brink of being rescued from Egypt, but it also looked forward to the fulfillment of the promise that they would cross the Jordan into the land God offered them. The Lord's Supper does the same thing. When we celebrate it, we look back to what Jesus has already accomplished, we acknowledge what Jesus is doing now, and we anticipate what Jesus will do in the time to come.

Thus, *remembering* both roots us in the past and points us toward a future, and the result directly affects our relationships in the present. In looking back, we are reminded of God's great love for the world, shown in Jesus' death and resurrection. In looking ahead, we see the wholeness that God intends for all the peoples of the world. Our calling in the present is to shape our relationships with God and others in such a way as to reflect the divine love we remember and the glory we anticipate.

2. *Freedom.* One of the things Jesus accomplished theologically for us is a new exodus. The parallels between the Exodus account and the Gospel descriptions of the life, death, and

resurrection of Jesus—particularly in the celebration of that
Passover meal that we know as the Last Supper—are deliber-
ate. We are supposed to hear the echoes of the former event
in the latter.

When we celebrate the Lord's Supper, we proclaim that
Christ brought us freedom from bondage, just as the exodus
event brought freedom from bondage for the Hebrews. The
bread of Christ, which gives us spiritual nourishment, recalls
the manna in the wilderness, from which the Hebrews
received daily physical sustenance. The cup, the blood of
Christ, parallels the blood of the covenant. (See Appendix B
for more detail on this.) Finally, the largest and greatest parallel is that the angel of death passes over once again, only this
time the angel passes permanently. The threat of death is gone
forever. Whatever power death had is no more—not just for a
single night, but for eternity.

The New Testament often speaks of Christ's accomplish-
ment in terms of our freedom from the bondage of sin and
death. Another way to word this is to say that in Christ we have
been set free to wholeness and life. We have been freed to enter
and maintain the *agape* relationships to which we are called.

3. *Hospitality.* In the earliest days of Israel's celebration of
covenant meals, the emphasis does not seem to be so much on
the type of animal killed or the way it was slaughtered as on
the meal itself. The meal was important as a concrete symbol
of the new relationship in which both parties now become like
family to one another. People did not sit down to eat together
unless (1) a host was offering hospitality to a guest, who was
then honor-bound not to harm the host, (2) two allies were
sharing a meal, or (3) it was a family mealtime.

More than that, sharing a meal with someone, even a passing stranger, obligated one as host to extend protection to the
person. Sitting at the meal together when ratifying a covenant
was a solid sign and seal of the new relationship being established. Through that act, one party said to the other, "I will

trust you. I will agree to protect you and to be there for you in the way that family is."

We understand Christ to be our host at the Table, to which we come by his invitation. This act of divine hospitality then becomes the model by which we are to welcome others, both at the Table and away from it. Such hospitality has profound implications for the church today, as Marjorie Thompson points out when she writes, "As we learn to receive God's hospitality to us, we will become more hospitable to God, to each other, and to our fellow creatures. This will make us a different kind of community. Others will see something enticing in us. Perhaps they will even say "See how they love one another!"[5]

4. *Belonging.* We have already discussed how a covenant actually establishes a relationship that amounts to a new family system. In Christ, God actually brings us into the divine family in a way that makes us siblings and coheirs with Christ! We move from being a nameless people to being children of God. We are claimed and named by God, who gives us a new identity. We will explore this transformation more thoroughly in chapter 4.

Hospitality

"Hospitality in biblical times was understood to be a way of meeting and receiving holy presence. Although providing hospitality was risky, it was a risk taken in faith. After all, the stranger just might be an angel—a messenger of God!"
— Thompson, 120–21

COVENANT RELATIONSHIPS IN CHRISTIAN LIFE TODAY

In looking back over what the Bible says about covenant relationships, we can see four implications for modern Christians. Briefly put, these are as follows:

1. *We are called to loving relationships.* Jesus' teaching on the greatest commandments makes clear that we are to love God, neighbor, and self. We are not to have just any love, however, but a love that grows out of and reflects the divine love God has shown to us. As 1 John 4:11 puts it, "Beloved, since God loved us so much, we also ought to love one another." Whether one thinks here of *hesed* or *agape*, the point is the same: We are to extend to God and one another the same steadfast, unwavering, and unconditional love that God always has for us.

> ### *Ephesians 4:31–32*
>
> "Put away from you all bitterness and wrath and anger and wrangling and slander, together with all malice, and be kind to one another, tenderhearted, forgiving one another, as God in Christ has forgiven you."

2. *We are called to responsible relationships.* Make no mistake: unconditional love does not mean blind love. Just as God holds us accountable while still loving us, so we are to do for others. Divine love demands that we speak against destructive behavior in others and work for wholeness on their behalf. We are also, of course, called to act responsibly by monitoring our own behavior as well.

3. *We are called to hospitable relationships.* God has designed human beings so that we are only complete in the company of others. Granted, some do better with more "alone time" than others do, and certain spiritual practitioners seek solitude as a way of life, yet we are communal creatures by nature. The challenge we face is that not everyone is easy to like or to welcome into our community. Nevertheless, God asks us to extend the same invitation to relationship to *all* people that God extends to us.

4. *We are called to transforming relationships.* If God is at the heart of all our relationships, then we should expect change for the better, both in ourselves and in others. In looking at what can happen when we let ourselves be "led by the Spirit" in our relationships, Shirley Guthrie says:

The Holy Spirit . . . calls, holds together, and sends out a new reconciled and reconciling community called the church; works in the world to create a whole new humanity and a whole new creation. When the Spirit breaks in old ways of thinking and living are left behind and new ways of thinking and living begin to take over. Old boring, oppressive, and dead social structures and institutions are transformed into exciting new, liberating ones. It may not happen all at once, but when the Holy Spirit comes there is the dawn of a new day, hope for a new and different future, and courage and strength to move toward it.[6]

The above implications describe the types of relationships we can have as children of God. They also, in a sense, paint a picture of life in God's community when it lives up to its full potential. As we know all too well, however, our ability to experience the promises and blessings of covenant relations can be affected by the choices we make. The next chapter discusses the concept of *choice* in more detail.

❦❦❦❦❦

QUESTIONS FOR REFLECTION

1. Which of the four aspects of the new covenant in Christ most speaks to you? Why? What other aspects would you add to this list?

2. What covenant relationships do you have in your life? How do you understand God to be present in them?

3. To what extent do these relationships exemplify the four characteristics listed in the last section above?

4. In what way is God's covenant with the community of faith an ongoing, dynamic part of your life and the life of your congregation?

5. What difference does "remembering" make in your relationship to God?

KEY LEARNINGS

- As Christians, we are created for and called to relationships.
- The primary means by which the Bible describes the type of relationship we are to have with God and others is in terms of *covenant*.
- Covenant relationships have one primary goal: to establish a *shalom* relationship where there was not one before.
- The new covenant in Christ includes remembrance, freedom, hospitality, and belonging.
- In the new covenant in Christ, we are called to relationships that are loving, responsible, hospitable, and transforming.

3

Called to Choice

From beginning to end, the Bible assures us that God has a holistic vision for creation that will be attained one day. In the meantime, we live in a less-than-perfect world, in which we struggle to live as God's covenant people.

Precisely because of this, the Bible underscores the importance of *choice* within the covenant relationship. This is not meant to say that by our own choice we can create divine covenants or destroy them. That prerogative belongs to God alone. Neither does it mean that God's blessings and promises have power only if we choose to accept them. God is not that limited.

Rather, I think the function of human choice goes back, in some ways, to the discussion in chapter 1 regarding *perspective*. Imagine that we have a number of lenses, with varying degrees of distortion, through which we can view the world. The Bible suggests that which lens we use is a matter of choice. Even more, the Bible clearly indicates that our ability to relate rightly with God and others depends a great deal on the resulting perspective. If we view our relationship with God and others through a clear and focused lens, the Bible suggests, then we will see God's covenant promises and blessings at work everywhere, and we will become transformed in a way that lets us participate fully in God's ongoing work in the world. If we view our relationship with God and others through an opaque and distorted lens, however, we will see little or no evidence of God's presence, and we will run the risk of never knowing what we are missing.

> ### Ephesians 5:1–2
>
> "Therefore be imitators of God, as beloved children, and live in love, as Christ loved us and gave himself up for us, a fragrant offering and sacrifice to God."

We see the importance of both *choice* and *perspective* in three different stories from the Old Testament, all of which relate to the people's entry into the promised land.

A MATTER OF CHOICE

One of the best examples of how God relates to us through choice is in Deuteronomy 30:11–20, in which Moses addresses the people just before they cross the Jordan into the promised land. They have come through an entire wilderness to get this far, and their long journey is almost over. First, Moses reminds them of everything God has done and everything God has asked of them in return. He hopes remembering these experiences will help the people look at their current situation through eyes of faith that see God's power and love fully at work on their behalf. Even more, Moses hopes that, as a natural response to this perspective, the people will be moved to choose covenant life with God. To help encourage the people to make this choice, Moses says:

> Surely, this commandment that I am commanding you today is not too hard for you, nor is it too far away. It is not in heaven, that you should say, "Who will go up to heaven for us, and get it for us so that

we may hear it and observe it?" Neither is it beyond
the sea, that you should say, "Who will cross to the
other side of the sea for us, and get it for us so that we
may hear it and observe it?" No, the word is very near
to you; it is in your mouth and in your heart for you
to observe. (Deut. 30:11–14)

Note that, according to Moses, God has already made a
response possible. Whatever it takes to live out the covenant
relationship God has already put in the people's mouths and
hearts. The same is true for us. It's a cop-out to say of the
Christian life, "It's too hard; I'll never be able to live up to it."
That's a faulty perception. We can love as God intends because
God will see to it that we can.

There is more, however. After Moses reassures the people
that the covenant is doable, he goes on to lead the people to a
choice. His sermon makes sense, though, only if one takes into
account the original Hebrew, because, throughout, Moses
uses two different Hebrew words for land. The first is *adamah*.
This word means dirt, ground, or dust, and it has no particular theological significance. The second word is *aretz* (or
eretz), which carries the sense of a land, territory, or nation
with boundaries that set it apart from other areas. When the
Old Testament writers talk about the promised land, they use
aretz. It's a word chock-full of theological meaning.

Keeping this in mind, look at what Moses says next:

See, I have set before you today life and prosperity,
death and adversity. If you obey the commandments
of the LORD your God that I am commanding you
today, by loving the LORD your God, walking in his
ways, and observing his commandments, decrees,
and ordinances, then you shall live and become
numerous, and the LORD your God will bless you in
the land [*aretz*] that you are entering to possess. But
if your heart turns away and you do not hear, but are
led astray to bow down to other gods and serve them,
I declare to you today that you shall perish; you shall

not live long in the land [*adamah*] that you are crossing the Jordan to enter and possess. I call heaven and earth to witness against you today that I have set before you life and death, blessings and curses. Choose life so that you and your descendants may live, loving the LORD your God, obeying him, and holding fast to him; for that means life to you and length of days, so that you may live in the land [*adamah*] that the LORD swore to give to your ancestors, to Abraham, to Isaac, and to Jacob. (Deut. 30:15–20)

We expect *aretz* in the last verse, but the writer uses *adamah*. Why? Because the people haven't chosen to enter into the covenant relationship yet. Until they do, the space across the Jordan is not *aretz*; it's just so much dirt. In essence, Moses uses *adamah* to startle the people into awareness. It is as if he is saying, "God has made you a promise. God has said there is *aretz* there for you. If you don't want to accept what it means to live in God's *aretz*, fine; that's your choice. You will cross the Jordan regardless and God's promise will still be real—but you will find only *adamah* on the other side. That is all that a perspective outside the covenant relationship will let you see."

The people are presented with a choice. If they enter into a genuine relationship with God, they will be able to see and experience the promise and blessings that go with it. Without the relationship with God, all they will have is dust—the same dust to which we return when we die. Moses deliberately sets *aretz* and its association with abundance in opposition to *adamah* and its association with death. He isn't kidding when he says, "I have set before you life and death" (v. 19). He does not necessarily mean physical death. After all, the people will cross the Jordan just fine and not drown in it. But what will happen to them in their spirit will be death nonetheless. That is the choice they have.

We face the same choice all the time. As Christians, we are

called to recommit ourselves to God and to covenant living at every moment of every day. Our chances of doing so grow higher when we keep a perspective that lets us see God at work in our lives and in the world around us. As long as we can hold a genuine awareness and thankfulness for the multiple blessings we have, it becomes a lot easier to respond appropriately.

OVERCOMING OUR RELUCTANCE

It seems a "no-brainer" that we would choose life over death or blessings over meaninglessness, but such responses are not always easy on a spiritual level. After all, a relationship with God offers us immeasurable hope, but it also comes with challenges—and that can be daunting.

> ### Our Response
>
> "But obedience is best understood as a response of gratitude and love to a gracious and loving God whose requirements are for the sake of creation. Furthermore, the God who calls us to obedience is the same One who has first freed us for obedience and who is able and ready to forgive our disobedience. God empowers obedience, encouraging and enabling us to live gratefully and responsively in relation to God's purposes and promises. In this way, obedience is true freedom." — Dykstra, 28

I am reminded of a woman I know who faced a significant career opportunity. She received an offer for what was, in many ways, her dream job. She was excited about the potential she saw if she said yes to the invitation: There was more money, a beautiful office, shorter hours, and a job that related directly to what she loved to do.

Yet this woman hesitated to say yes. The job involved moving to a new city, and she dreaded the idea of packing up belongings that had accumulated over twenty-three years. It also meant working with new people, and who knew if she would get along with them all? Her old job was no longer particularly satisfying, but it was comfortable and familiar. The new job sounded great, but what if she didn't like it after all? She was genuinely torn between desire for the blessings held out before her and reluctance to pay the cost or take the risks to get them.

I think the Hebrew people must have been in a similar dilemma as they anticipated moving from the wilderness area into the promised land at last. They knew from the reports of their spies that the land was beautiful and bountiful. They knew from Moses that it held the promise of a unique relationship with God. They had every reason to believe, intellectually, that once they were in the land—living in houses they didn't have to build, drinking from wells they didn't have to dig, and eating from gardens they didn't have to plant (Deut. 6:10–12)—they would not regret their choice. But they weren't in the land yet, and the spies' reports had also described fortified cities to be conquered and giants to be beaten. So they found themselves reluctant to claim something they saw as a great blessing.

Numbers 13:30–14:10 tells how two men, Caleb and Joshua, challenged the people to change their perspective. These two could speak with some authority because they were among the original spies: They had seen the land's challenges for themselves. Unlike the other spies, however, they were not daunted by the experience. They chose to focus on the power of God instead of the obstacles in the land, and that made all the difference. They did not delude themselves about the challenges at hand, but neither did they give in to despair or hopelessness. Their perspective, rooted in faith, gave them the courage to reach out for the blessing God offered.

The people would have none of it, though. They had heard the reports (and opinions) of the other spies, and they saw entry into the promised land as an act of suicide. They were so afraid, in fact, that when Caleb and Joshua persisted in trying to change their minds, the people threatened to stone them (Num. 14:10)!

We have the advantage of knowing the end of the story. We know that eventually, under Joshua's leadership, the people did cross the Jordan and move into the promised land. So what happened to help them overcome their reluctance?

The answer lies in the second half of Numbers 14:10, just after we see the rebellious mob at the point of violence. As the crowd threatens to stone Caleb and Joshua, "Then the glory of the LORD appeared at the tent of meeting to all the Israelites." In other words, God came into their midst. There would be consequences to face as a result of their actions, but God was present with them anyway. This is the same God who, generations later, would tell the people through the prophet Hosea after similar provocation:

> I will not execute my fierce anger;
> I will not again destroy Ephraim;
> for I am God and no mortal,
> the Holy One in your midst,
> and I will not come in wrath.
> (Hos. 11:9)

The living presence of God in the midst of the community of faith—then and now—is always the best catalyst for life-giving change. Face to face with God, it's amazing how fast our priorities and our perspective can shift back in line with the divine plan!

ONE TOE IN THE BLESSING

You know how some people cannot enter a pool of water without first testing it with one toe? There are people who approach covenant relationships like that. This is what we see in the story of the first Passover celebrated in the promised land (Joshua 5). The people had finally crossed the Jordan, and they camped at a place called Gilgal. Four days later, they celebrated the Passover there. Think about this. The first significant religious event of the community of faith after they cross the Jordan and metaphorically have one toe in the promised land is one in which they remember both the occasion of the exodus and God's promise to their ancestors that they would reach this place. Imagine what that Passover must have been like!

As they celebrated that day, barely inside the boundaries of the promised land, they not only looked back to the past. They also looked forward to the continued fulfillment of God's promise, which would come as they moved farther into the land and claimed the *shalom* God planned for them.

This is the same thing promised to us in the covenant in Jesus. Like the people who had just crossed the Jordan and who barely stood inside the promised land, in Jesus we stand just inside the promise God has for us—we stand on the edge of God's new creation. We are not all the way in yet, but we are there. Moreover, every time we come to the Table to celebrate, it is like celebrating that Passover at Gilgal. We celebrate the fact that we have made it as far as we have inside God's promise; we celebrate the degree to which God's promises

> ### Privilege and Responsibility
>
> "God elected Israel to be the covenant people, but this election to privilege was an election to corresponding responsibility. When this responsibility was ignored, election placed Israel under judgment. We are reminded of the words of Jesus: 'From everyone to whom much has been given, much will be required' (Luke 12:48)." — Rhodes, 131

have been fulfilled so far. We also acknowledge that there are challenges ahead, and we still have a way to go.

Certainly the people at Gilgal had a lot to celebrate, and yet they still had much to face. To be sure, there was the promise of the milk and honey flowing, but there were also many legitimate reports of the fighting they would have to do in order to claim the promise. Hostile groups were still ahead, as were the fortified cities and the giants. So the people, having been tempted enough by the beauties of the land to "dip their toe" into it, now wonder if they really want to go farther. Perhaps they'll be most comfortable just staying on the edge, right where they are!

What we see is that God does not allow such easy choices. The day after the people celebrated the Passover, the manna stopped. The people were forced to live off the fruit of the land, and this eventually was going to mean moving deeper into the territory. From one perspective, this can be seen as proof that God continued to care and provide for the people. By stopping the manna and forcing the Hebrews to seek food from the land itself, God kept the divine provision from becoming an excuse to postpone claiming the promised land. God, in essence, pushed the toe-dippers in!

As Christians, we live with a similar kind of tension. We stand inside the realm of God that Jesus initiated on earth, but we also recognize that there is a lot of that realm still to unfold before us. Our journey is by no means over, and we will surely continue to meet obstacles along the way. Thus, it is sometimes tempting to think about setting up camp right where we are—to settle for what we have, because seeking more involves risk. In these times, it helps to remember that God is not above pushing us all the way in if that's what we really need.

For those who serve the church—whether as pastors, teachers, or in other positions of leadership—this has tremendous ramifications. These are the people who stand on the brink of God's new land and fight the temptation to go no farther. These are our Calebs, the ones who tell the community honestly about the dangers ahead, but who also perceive joy in the beautiful blessings to be had. They are our Joshuas—the ones who encourage us, cajole us, yell at us, cry with us, love us, hold us, push us, pull us, walk beside us, and keep us moving deeper into the promised land. The end result? As we will see in the next chapter, it is no less than the establishment of a new identity as children of God.

❦❦❦❦❦

QUESTIONS FOR REFLECTION

1. What are some of the blessings in your life for which you are grateful? How do these blessings move you to respond?

2. What helps you keep a positive perspective in life?

3. Think of a specific time when you responded positively to a call from God despite some reluctance. In what ways did you feel adequate for this calling? In what way did you feel inadequate? What happened?

4. Who are your Calebs and Joshuas? For whom have you fulfilled this role?

KEY LEARNINGS

- As Christians, we are called to continually recommit to God and to covenant living.
- A healthy perspective, one in which we continually see God at work in our lives and in the world around us, can help us do this.
- We are sometimes hesitant to accept God's blessings because of perceived cost or risk to ourselves.
- Staying in touch with the presence of God can help overcome this reluctance, as can listening to the encouragement of others in the faith community.

4

Called to a New Identity

The relationship to which God calls us is one that leads to genuine transformation. The seemingly simple promise "I will be your God, and you shall be my people" rings with God's power to bring about change in radical ways. Indeed, at the heart of this promise is the conviction that God can (and will) give us a completely new identity, one that leaves us free to live into God's grand plan. The primary way that Ephesians explains this change in status is through the imagery of *adoption*.

In the days of the early Christian church, Roman law gave the male head of a household the power to adopt another. The adopted person then received the full rights and privileges of any other family member, just as if the person had been born to them. Former circumstances no longer mattered: Even if the adopted one came from the poorest of circumstances and had no value whatsoever in the eyes of society before, now that person was

> ### *Ephesians 1:5*
>
> "He destined us for adoption as his children through Jesus Christ, according to the good pleasure of his will."

considered indistinguishable, legally and socially, from those born into the family. The writer of Ephesians wants to underscore that the one God we all profess is the same God who has granted each of us such status, even to the extent of being full and uncontested heirs. When we accept this role and identity, we accept the corresponding call to be part of the family business: bringing God's vision to fruition however and whenever we can.

CHILDREN OF GOD

Think about meeting someone for the first time. What information do you tend to exchange with the other in order to get acquainted? Do you describe yourself in terms of where and with whom you work? Do you speak in terms of family ("I'm married to . . . ," "I'm the parent of . . . ," etc.)? Do you talk about those you might know in common? Do you mention something about your church? Chances are, you do at least one of these things.

We tend to define ourselves in terms of our relationships. My name alone tells you almost nothing about me, but if I tell you about my family or my job or my church, then you begin to know something about me and who I am. The whole heart of our identity as a Christian community is in the belonging that we have in Christ.

In the Bible, God's transforming power is illustrated by the granting of a new name when a covenant relationship is established. Abram and Jacob, who became Abraham and Israel, are two great examples of this in the Old Testament. In the New Testament, the renaming of Peter and Paul likewise represent transformation. *Renaming* indicates indisputably that covenant brings one into a new identity.

I have had real appreciation of this lately. A couple of years ago, my husband and I were trying to get a copy of his birth certificate, so we went online to do a search of the state's records. Sure enough, we found the forms we needed, and we printed them out to complete and fax to the state office. Once we actually started to fill out the forms, however, we realized that we did not know how to proceed. The form asked for the mother's full name, the father's full name, and the child's full name—but my husband was adopted as an infant. We did not know if the form was asking for information on his birth parents or his adoptive parents. We did not know if the form required his birth name or his adopted name. We literally did not know his identity at that point, and we did not know what to do. When we called the state office for clarification, they explained that they wanted my husband's adopted name and the names of his adoptive parents—"because," they said, "as far as our office is concerned, from the moment of adoption that relationship was retroactive to the moment of his birth." Think about that.

The same thing happens in our relationship with God. God says, in essence, "Once you enter into covenant with me, it is retroactive not only to your birth but to the birth of all creation. From the moment there was anything, I have been your God, and you have been my child." Our new identity is now counted as having been forever—and God promises it will continue to be forever.

Perhaps this is why the letter to the Ephesians so often refers to God as "Father." While this language may be offensive or uncomfortable to some, it is essential to the language of adoption, as we shall see.

ADOPTION IN THE OLD TESTAMENT

Adoption as such does not occur in the Old Testament. In fact, there is no Hebrew word to indicate this kind of legal action. The closest parallel is a phrase: to take someone as a son or daughter. While this establishes a certain kind of special relationship, it does not eliminate the child's connection to the birth parents, nor does it equate to the full rights of adoption that we know today.

The lack of an adoption practice is not that surprising, given the Jewish understanding of family and the importance of maintaining a clear connection to one's bloodline. In no case was a child to be taken into another family and given a new identity. The father (and the family line as a whole) were perceived as gaining a sort of immortality through the ongoing existence of the family name in each subsequent generation. Loss of the family name amounted to the loss of the entire family's identity.

Moreover, other laws in the culture made adoption unnecessary. Men addressed the problem of childlessness by taking multiple wives; childless widows could invoke the law of levirate marriage, which obligated a male in-law to marry her and seek to give her children. There is even some indication that wealthy women could claim their slaves' children as their own in certain cases, as we will discuss later.

At the same time, there is evidence that the Hebrews knew of the practice of adoption from other cultures, especially as this related to the adoption of slaves for the purpose of establishing an heir. This custom was common enough in other parts of the ancient Near East to appear in the law codes of Babylon, Nuzi, and Ugarit—all of which could have impacted the social world of the Hebrews. Accordingly, many scholars think the ancient laws of those other cultures lie behind biblical texts in which a slave is named as heir (Gen. 16:1–4; 21:1–10; 30:1–13).[1]

In addition, there are examples in the Old Testament of children being raised by people other than their birth parents, and the relationship is often described as one of parent and child. For example, when Pharaoh's daughter pulls Moses from the river and decides to rear him as her own, the text says, "She took him as her son" (Exod. 2:10). Her first act in the parental role is to then name the child (v. 10). Likewise, after the death of Esther's mother and father, her cousin Mordecai raised her "as his own daughter" (Esth. 2:7).

Moreover, children could be granted the status of sons and heirs, even when their own parents were still living, as Genesis 48 shows. In this text, Jacob has finally been reunited with his son Joseph, who had been sold into slavery by his brothers many years before. In order to ensure the prosperity of Joseph's line, Jacob claims Joseph's two sons, Ephraim and Manasseh, as his own and gives them status equal to that of his own two firstborn sons, Reuben and Simeon (Gen. 48:5). The fact that Ephraim and Manasseh were placed on Jacob's knees (or lap) may indicate a physical action that was part of a traditional adoption ceremony (v. 12). By taking the two boys as his own, Jacob accomplishes two things: He guarantees their portion of the inheritance, and he ensures that his own name will be perpetuated (v. 16).

In addition, one could sometimes establish a slave as one's heir. This seems to be the case in Genesis 15:2–3 when Abraham indicates that Eliezer of Damascus, a slave born in his household, is his designated heir. Eliezer could inherit only if Abraham had claimed him as a son and granted him that status, so many commentators think this verse may refer to an adoption practice similar to those described in ancient documents from Nuzi and Ugarit, two sites to the north of Israel. Something similar may be implied in 1 Chronicles 2:34, in which the sonless Sheshan gives his daughter in marriage to Jarha, an Egyptian slave, so that their son might become his heir.

The act of establishing someone else's child as one's own was not limited to men. Genesis 16:2 describes how Sarah asked Abraham to father a child with Hagar, Sarah's slave, so that Sarah could then claim the child as her own. Likewise, in Genesis 30:1–13, we see both Rachel and Leah, two sisters married to Jacob, using their slaves to birth children they can then claim as their own. (Note that in each case Rachel and Leah are the ones who name the child, a sign of their role as mother.) Rachel's reference to the slave's bearing a child "upon my knees . . . that I too may have children through her" (Gen. 30:3) has been taken as an ancient ritual of adoption.

Despite the rarity of adoption as a social institution in Israel, however, there was a strong theological sense that the Hebrew people had been adopted by God and elevated to the role of "child" (see Isa. 1:2; Jer. 3:19; Hos. 11:1). Moreover, this role included status as God's heir, in the sense that the people are often referred to as those who will "inherit" the land that God has set aside (see, for example, Exod. 32:13; Lev. 20:24; Jer. 12:14).

"The word *plan (oikonomia)* has a second meaning that will be important in Ephesians. The word might be translated 'rules for the household' or 'management of the household.' The notion of God running the world as if it were God's own house and all people members of that house will surface in two ways in the letter. First, in 2:19 the author declares that we who were once aliens are now 'citizens with the saints and also members of the household of God.' The image here is one of having fallen under God's parental care. The world is no longer an alien evil place, but a household where God nurtures us and protects us. Second, membership in this household involves certain obligations and duties. These duties are played out in the many ethical imperatives in the letter." —Donelson, 65

ADOPTION IN GREECE

In the Greek world, the earliest written evidence of formal adoption comes from the second century B.C., although there do seem to have been equivalent ceremonies in earlier centuries. The purpose of adoption seems always to have been to establish an heir who would care for one in old age and then inherit one's belongings. In parts of Greece, this could be done even if there were already natural children who, by rights, one would expect to inherit everything. In other areas, such as Athens, however, a person could adopt an heir only if there were no children. In each case, however, certain elements were present:

1. The adoption ceremony took place before an assembly of citizens and/or local heads of government. In other words, it was not private.
2. The name of the adopted person, whether child or adult, did not change.
3. The adopted person immediately entered into the full rights and responsibilities of the new relationship. The rights included a claim to inheritance, as was almost always made clear in a will that was presented at the adoption ceremony, and the responsibilities included an ironclad financial obligation to care for the adopted parents until their death.
4. The adopted person was almost always a free citizen; the adoption of slaves was rare.

ADOPTION IN THE ROMAN WORLD

Many of these aspects carried over into the Roman practice of adoption as well. Although very similar to adoption in the Greek culture, Roman adoption was divided into two types. The first was known as *adoptio*, and it represented the adoption of a person, male or female, who was still under the authority of a living father. In the ceremony, which took place before a high-placed government official, the birth father enacted a transference of power to the adoptive father. Roman women, who did not have authority over their own children, were not allowed to adopt.

The second type of adoption, *adrogatio* (or *arrogatio*), was limited to males who were not under a father's power. There were other rules and restrictions as well:

1. The adoptive father could not have children or expect to sire any.
2. The adoptive father had to be older than the person being adopted.
3. If the adopted son was a father himself, then his children became the legal grandchildren of the adopting man.
4. The property of the adopted son immediately became the property of the adopting father.

In both types of adoption, the same end was achieved. A legal relationship of parent and child was established, just as if there had been a natural birth in a marriage. An adopted child was counted as a brother or sister to any natural-born children the father might have, and he or she gained both the right to the father's name and the right to inherit (insofar as gender allowed).

ADOPTION IN THE NEW TESTAMENT

The apostle Paul took the common social practice of adoption that he knew from Roman culture and gave it a unique theological spin. Indeed, in the New Testament, the imagery of adoption occurs only in the Pauline letters, and it is always in the context of our standing as children of God.

> The book of Ephesians uses the language of "Father" for God because, in the Roman world, only male heads of households could adopt an heir.

The earliest example is from the letter to the Galatians, which says that God sent Jesus Christ to redeem us, "so that we might receive adoption as children" (4:5). This new status as children of God allows us to address God as Jesus did, using "Abba," the familiar and affectionate Aramaic equivalent of "Papa" or "Daddy" (4:6; see Mark 14:36). Moreover, our new status grants us full rights as God's "heirs" (Gal. 4:7).

In Romans 8, Paul expands on this concept in a rather convoluted statement. He says first that when we call on God as "Abba," it is through the prompting of the Spirit. Then he adds that such prompting is proof that the Spirit is in us—and the Spirit's presence is proof of our adoption as God's children (vv. 14–16). Then, in order to make our status even clearer, Paul goes on to say that we are not only God's heirs but are "joint heirs with Christ" (v. 17).

Adoption in Ephesians

All of this has bearing on how we are to understand the view of adoption found throughout Ephesians. The writer of Ephesians, whether Paul or someone who knew him well, wanted to convey the significance of this adopted status to the Gentiles who first received this letter. For them in particular, the new identity as child of God represented a radical break with everything they had known or done.

The first chapter of Ephesians is designed to underscore the importance of this new identity, and verses 11–14 are critical in this regard. Regarding these verses, one scholar says:

Ephesians 1:11–14

"In Christ we have also obtained an inheritance, having been destined according to the purpose of him who accomplishes all things according to his counsel and will, so that we, who were the first to set our hope on Christ, might live for the praise of his glory. In him you also, when you had heard the word of truth, the gospel of your salvation, and had believed in him, were marked with the seal of the promised Holy Spirit; this is the pledge of our inheritance toward redemption as God's own people, to the praise of his glory."

This short [section] makes a distinctive contribution to the main purpose of the letter. It not only is calculated to inspire the readers with confidence that God's plan will not miscarry en route to its finale; it demonstrates to Gentile believers how they—with Israel's remnant—are part and parcel of the new people which has inseparable roots in the Israel of the old covenant.[2]

Throughout Ephesians, we find seven things the writer wants to make clear to the original audience, and each of these insights holds true for us as well:

1. Our adoption is through Jesus Christ. It is our relationship with him that makes our adoption possible (1:5).
2. Our adoption takes place because of God's love for us. It is an act of "the good pleasure of his will" (v. 5) and "his glorious grace" (v. 6).
3. Our adoption assures us of an inheritance (v. 11), and that inheritance is redemption as God's people (v. 14).
4. Our adoption saved us from death and "made us alive together with Christ" (2:5). Moreover, because we are now counted as heirs, God has "raised us up with him and seated us with him in the heavenly places in Christ Jesus" (v. 6).
5. Our adoption has not only given us life, but community. It has changed us from "strangers and aliens" into "citizens with the saints and also members of the household of God" (2:19).
6. Our adoption is the heart of the good news of the gospel, and it has been part of God's goal from before creation (3:5–6).
7. Our adoption has transformed us into a new creation, "created according to the likeness of God in true righteousness and holiness" (4:24).

What a wonderful list of privileges and gifts we have here! As with adoption in the Greek and Roman cultures, however, so our own status as adopted children comes with responsibilities. Accordingly, we can add one final point to the above list: Our adoption is the reason we are to "lead a life worthy of the calling to which [we] have been called" (4:1). The next chapter will look more closely at the relationship between our status as God's children and our call to live a certain way.

⋙⋙⋙

QUESTIONS FOR REFLECTION

1. What does it mean to you to be a child of God and a coheir with Christ? What difference, if any, does it make for your life as a Christian?

2. What insights into these images do you gain through studying the ancient cultures?

3. What adoption stories do you know that shed light on this image as it applies to Christians?

4. What do you value most about belonging to the family of God?

KEY LEARNINGS

- As Christians, we are called to be children of God, a status that God grants to us.
- In the Roman world, the male head of a household could adopt an heir. The adopted child had full rights within the family, just as if she or he had been born there.
- The writer of Ephesians uses the image of adoption to describe the new life and identity we have as children of God.
- Our adoption in Christ, which has been part of God's plan all along, assures us of redemption, provides us with a community, and transforms us into a new creation.

5

Called to a Way of Life

One of the more familiar images from the Bible is that of the
"path" or the "way." In the biblical languages, as in English,
these words carry two meanings. On a literal level, they indicate a trail or road that one follows when going from one place
to another. Figuratively, each term refers to a spiritual course
that one follows throughout the journey of life. In both cases,
sticking to the chosen path requires a certain amount of self-
discipline, especially if the terrain gets a little rough or if dis-
tractions tempt us to go off in another direction, but it is worth
the effort. After all, sticking to the path is what gets us to our
final destination.

Perhaps that is why the writer of Ephesians uses similar
imagery when he urges believers "*to lead* a life worthy of the
calling to which you have been called" (4:1, italics added);
the actual Greek phrase literally means "to walk" or "to
make one's way." As a spiritual metaphor, of course, the term
also means to conduct one's life according to a certain stan-
dard. It indicates adherence to a guiding principle so perva-
sive it permeates everything we do. Only by acting in ways
that are truly consistent with our new identity as members

of God's household, the writer implies, are we "worthy" of our calling.

The plea in Ephesians 4:1 is preliminary to what follows in verses 2–6. There the writer offers a brief yet beautiful description of the characteristics we should expect to see in a life consistent with our new identity as members of God's household. This list encapsulates the way of life to which we are called.

> ### Ephesians 4:1–3
>
> "I therefore, the prisoner in the Lord, beg you to lead a life worthy of the calling to which you have been called, with all humility and gentleness, with patience, bearing with one another in love, making every effort to maintain the unity of the Spirit in the bond of peace."

Before looking at these verses in detail, however, it will be helpful to review their setting in the book of Ephesians as a whole. In this carefully crafted letter, key images thread in and out of the overall discussion, and we can understand Ephesians 4:1–6 better if we first look at what precedes it.

THE BACKGROUND TO EPHESIANS

The letter labeled as "to the Ephesians" may not have been, at least not exclusively. Because the oldest manuscripts lack the phrase "who are in Ephesus" after the opening address of "To the saints"—and because the letter does not contain any greetings to specific people, even though Paul spent over two years in Ephesus (Acts 19:10)—many scholars think the letter was originally meant to circulate among the various churches of the area as a general statement on the Christian life. If this is so, then it may speak more directly to our congregations today than some texts that are more closely tied to a historical situation.

Another mystery is whether the letter was actually written by Paul. The language and vocabulary are different enough that some scholars call this into question. At the same time, the ideas in the letter are enough like Paul's own that, if it was not written by him, it must have been written by someone who knew him well.

Ephesians 1 begins by saying all things have happened according to God's plan and that we are a part of that plan. Here, God's grand vision is defined in terms of our transformation, in which we are "to be holy and blameless before [God] in love" (1:4). According to the writer of Ephesians, this is what God had planned for us even before creating the world. Moreover, God has planned from the beginning to unite everyone (and everything) in Christ's body, the church (v. 10).

In Ephesians 2, we see how God's ancient plan was beginning to come to fruition, specifically in the unity of Jews and Gentiles in Christ's church. The writer begins by reminding the audience that they were as good as dead in their old way of life. Now, however, not only are they fully alive, they have been elevated to special status. As the writer says:

> God, who is rich in mercy, out of the great love with
> which he loved us even when we were dead through
> our trespasses, made us alive together with Christ . . .
> and raised us up with him and seated us with him in
> the heavenly places in Christ Jesus. (Eph. 2:4–6)

The tremendous good news is this: These particular Christians, Gentile by birth, are no longer "aliens . . . strangers . . . far off" (vv. 12–13), because they have been "brought near by the blood of Christ" (v. 13). The dividing wall that kept Gentiles out of the sacred places where Israel alone interacted with God has now been destroyed by Christ, so that hostility between the groups is no more (v. 14).

Most interpreters say the imagery of the dividing wall comes from the Gospel accounts of Jesus' death. According to Matthew 27:51 and Mark 15:38, when Jesus died, "The curtain of the temple was torn in two, from top to bottom."[1] The curtain represented the barrier between us and God caused by sin, a barrier broken down by Jesus' death and resurrection. The writer of Ephesians says that the barrier that separated Jews and Gentiles was also destroyed at that time.

In an effort to describe the new Christian community that now exists, the writer uses four images. First, we are *one body* (Eph. 2:16). We are also all *citizens with the saints* in God's realm and, even more intimately, *members of the household of God* (v. 19). Finally, we are *a holy temple* in Christ (v. 21), a temple that is "a dwelling place for God" (v. 22).

In Ephesians 3, the writer ties together the points made in chapters 1 and 2. Here we read succinctly:

> In former generations this mystery was not made known to humankind, as it has now been revealed to his holy apostles and prophets by the Spirit: that is, the Gentiles have become fellow heirs, members of the same body, and sharers in the promise in Christ Jesus through the gospel. (3:5–6)

The first clause of the final section of the letter, Ephesians 4–6, has a loaded word: Therefore . . ." (4:1). This indicates that the next few verses and their call to Christian unity are actually building on something said earlier. Indeed, the full argument reaches back to the start of chapter 3, which reveals a divine mystery—that Jews and Gentiles together are full heirs to God's fulfilled promises. *Because* we are all heirs to "the promise in Christ Jesus through the gospel" (3:6), *therefore* we should act accordingly—and our appropriate response, as it is outlined in 4:2–6, involves worthiness, unity, and peace.

LIVING WORTHILY

As Ephesians 4:1 puts it, we are to "lead a life worthy of the calling to which [we] have been called." "Worthy" translates a

Greek word that originated in the marketplace; its first meaning related to weighing items with a set of counterbalancing scales to see if they were of equal value. In time, use of the word expanded to include relationships that were fitting or appropriate to a set of standards. Thus when the writer of Ephesians urges Christians to live worthy of "the calling to which you have been called" (v. 1), he pleads for behavior that is equal to or consistent with that calling. The passage does not suggest we can make ourselves worthy, only that we should respond to grace's call in appropriate ways.

The next verse lists some qualities of conduct that are fit for the Christian life: humility, gentleness, patience, and bearing with one another. The list is deceptively simple in that these traits, which seem easy enough to achieve on the surface, are nevertheless often lacking in the Christian community.

- *Humility* is based in a spirit of service that leads us to put others ahead of ourselves. It is more than setting aside pride; it involves true unselfishness.
- *Gentleness*, or meekness, as this word is translated in the Sermon on the Mount (Matt. 5:5), is an attitude toward others that grows out of divine love. It is the opposite of arrogance, anger, and impatience. As we see in Jesus' example, gentleness is *not* weakness.
- *Patience* in Greek literally means "long-suffering," and it is often used to describe the forbearance God shows to us. As a Christian trait, patience is a spiritual force rooted in our relationship with God; we are to have the same patience for others that God has for us.
- *Bearing with one another* involves accepting others, even when they are unpleasant, and refusing to let their behavior break the relationship. It can also refer to restraining oneself from acting in anger.

All these attributes are rooted in the kind of unconditional love Paul described in 1 Corinthians 13. Indeed, they are pivotal ways in which we express God's divine love to one another. Thus, these attitudes form the crux of the "worthy" life of Christians.

MAINTAINING UNITY

The real goal of walking in the Christian way is to do everything we can to "maintain the unity of the Spirit in the bond of peace" (v. 3). This is the ultimate aim of the Christian community. Note that we are not asked to *create* this unity; God has done that for us already. Our task is to promote and preserve this incredible gift that God has entrusted to us.

In fact, the word translated as "maintain" brings us back to the goal of humanity at the start of creation. There we were told to "keep" ("garrison" or "defend") God's creation; the equivalent word is used here to describe what we are to do with God's peace. We are to guard it as something precious and expend every effort to ensure its safety.

Given all the things that divide the church today, the call to maintain peaceful unity in the Spirit may seem next to impossible to us. The challenge was just as overwhelming in some ways for the early Christians in Ephesus. That is why Paul added the little creedal statement in verses 4–6. If we focus on our differences, the apostle seems to imply, we will never get anywhere. Instead, we must start with what we hold in common, because that is what ultimately holds us together: "one body and one Spirit, . . . one hope . . . , one Lord, one faith, one baptism, one God and Father of all, who is above all and through all and in all."

> ### Unity in Christ
>
> "It may seem strange for Paul to speak of unity in Christ as a fact and then call people to unity in Christ. But this should not seem strange. As Christians are always becoming what they are, so the church is always becoming what it is."
> — Rhodes, 353

These seven areas of unity lie at the core of all our faith experiences, uniting each of us into a common fellowship of faith. Let's look at them a little closer.

1. *There is one body.* The image of the church as Christ's body runs throughout Ephesians and finds special emphasis here. Like a view of the earth from space, in which the national and local boundaries drawn on maps cannot be seen, this perspective of the church does not see denominations or variations in practices—it sees only the person of Jesus Christ, who unites us in himself as one body.

2. *There is one Spirit.* The Holy Spirit, working throughout the whole body of Christ, enables us to maintain our unity. Moreover, through its power, we have access to God's revelations (Eph. 1:17; 3:5), we become "strengthened in [our] inner being with power" (3:16), and we gain access to the power of prayer (6:18).

3. *There is one hope.* The promise of Christ's return and the eventual redemption of all creation is the ultimate source of hope for us. As we look forward to these events, our hope takes on elements of patient waiting, expectation, and trust, and it also orients us with a new attitude toward the world.

> Some people think the writer used seven items deliberately because seven is the number for wholeness and completeness in the OT tradition. Given that the intended audience was Gentile, this may or may not have been the case. Either way, the creed is effective. As Ralph Martin points out:
>
> > "[I]ts simplicity is its strength, and it may be the focal point of ecumenical unity for which modern Christendom still is searching. When Christians come together across the dividing fences of their denominational allegiances they find they have more in common than they suspected. They meet not to create unity but to confess it."[2]

4. *There is one Lord.* The early Christians summed up the gospel with an extraordinarily brief creedal statement: "Jesus is Lord" (1 Cor. 12:3). Public confession of Jesus as Lord continues to be one of the requirements for new church members today. It is our belief that Jesus Christ is our Lord and Savior that grants us the name "Christian" in the first place.

5. *There is one faith.* "Faith" here most likely refers to the core set of beliefs and teachings regarding the gospel message that all Christians hold in common. Yet, as elsewhere in the New Testament, "faith" also refers to our personal relationship with and commitment to Jesus, and it links our love of Christ to love of neighbor (see 1 John 3:23).

6. *There is one baptism.* From the earliest beginnings of the church, entry into the body of Christ has been marked by baptism to signify our union with Christ in his death and resurrection. It is our sign and seal that God forgives sins and grants new life to those who believe. Moreover, in the Greek form, baptism refers both to the act itself and to the result—our immediate new status as brothers and sisters in Christ.

7. *There is one God.* This is the same God we worship as creator and sovereign, and whom we also dare approach in Christ as "Abba" (Rom. 8:15; Gal. 4:6). This is the one God who has called each of us to life in Christ, sent the Holy Spirit among us, and blessed us with the gifts of faith. This God who is "above all and through all and in all" (Eph. 4:6) is the ultimate source of our unity.

KEEPING PEACE

The unity to which we are called results in "the bond of peace" (Eph. 4:3). This language particularly relates to *reconciliation*, a theme that runs throughout Ephesians:

> The barrier that divided is broken down, and access to God previously a bone of contention between Gentiles and Jews is declared to stand open to all races. Moreover, the access works on a new plane, since it now betokens the horizontal communication that Christ makes possible. Cultures and classes that had been separated by walls of prejudice and tradition are now opened to one another, and the lines of connection and conversation are established. It is this twofold

imagery of a double reconciliation—to God and to our fellow human beings—that is the unique contribution of Ephesians and marks it out as one of the most timely New Testament documents for our day.[3]

Ephesians affirms and celebrates that we are truly bound together by what we hold in common as Christians. Moreover, it lifts up these points of unity as being integral to the way of life to which we are called. At the same time, Ephesians does not equate our unity with uniformity: It also celebrates the diversity of gifts that we bring to Christ's body, the church. The next two chapters explore this aspect of Christian life and its implications for our calling within God's overarching vision.

> ## Ephesians 4:4–6
>
> "There is one body and one Spirit, just as you were called to the one hope of your calling, one Lord, one faith, one baptism, one God and Father of all, who is above all and through all and in all."

❧❧❧❧❧❧

QUESTIONS FOR REFLECTION

1. What reconciliation between people have you seen God's grace achieve?

2. Paul says that God's plan for the fullness of time is "to gather up all things" in Christ's church, which is his body. What boundaries (race, age, gender, etc.) have you seen broken down in your congregation?

3. How do the qualities Paul lists in Ephesians 4:2–3 correspond to your ideas of a life worthy of Christ's calling? What would you add to that list? Why?

4. How does your church model the elements of Christian unity listed in vv. 4–6?

KEY LEARNINGS

- As Christians, we are called to "lead a life worthy of the calling to which [we] have been called" (Eph. 4:1).
- For the writer of Ephesians, the overall goal of that life is *reconciliation*, as shown in the plea to "maintain the unity of the Spirit in the bond of peace" (v. 3).
- The writer of Ephesians identifies seven points of unity for all Christians: one body, one Spirit, one hope, one Lord, one faith, one baptism, one God and Father of us all (vv. 4–6).
- We are truly bound together by what we hold in common as Christians.

6

Called to Competence

The way of life to which we are called as Christians includes participating in God's vision for the church through the use of our gifts and talents. Lest we think we have nothing to contribute (and hence no responsibility in this regard), Paul reassures us that "our competence is from God, who has made us competent to be ministers of a new covenant" (2 Cor. 3:5–6). This chapter and the next will focus on two parts of this statement: our competency and our ministry.

"Competent" can seem a somewhat boring way to describe our abilities through spiritual gifts. Perhaps that is because, in more common parlance, we associate "competent" with "adequate." It in-

> **Ephesians 4:7–8**
>
> "But each of us was given grace according to the measure of Christ's gift. Therefore it is said,
>
> > 'When he ascended on high he made captivity itself a captive;
> > he gave gifts to his people.'"

dicates a skill level that can get the job done on the minimal level of acceptability, without promising anything more.

Paul means far more when he uses the term, however. First, the Greek word indicates *sufficiency*, in the sense of having enough to accomplish an end. In the case of what we receive from God, this is never what is merely adequate. Rather, God gives us what is sufficient to accomplish serving the church and the world in the best way, so our efforts are whole and complete and in no way lacking.

Moreover, Paul clearly roots our competency in God's own power, grace, and sovereignty. In other words, Paul offers the comforting view that we can trust God's promise to make us competent for the tasks at hand because God indeed has the will and the power to do so.

WE ARE NOT ALONE

Think back to the previous chapter and its discussion on Ephesians 4:1–6. It is interesting to note that the very next verses move from what we have in common to our differences. In particular, verses 7–8 focus on the unique gifts we each have. Moreover, according to Ephesians 4:11–13:

> The gifts [Christ] gave were that some would be apostles, some prophets, some evangelists, some pastors and teachers, to equip the saints for the work of ministry, for building up the body of Christ, until all of us come to the unity of the faith and of the knowledge of the Son of God, to maturity, to the measure of the full stature of Christ.

At first glance, this list may seem somewhat exclusive, because it focuses on the roles of leadership that were present in the early church. A closer look reveals that the writer of Ephesians viewed these special positions as part of a larger whole, which includes all believers.

Ephesians 4:12 makes clear that the aim of these gifted

Ephesians identifies several leadership positions designed to help all members of the church grow in their competence for ministry. These are:

Apostles. This term usually refers to the original eyewitnesses of the resurrected Christ, who went on to become the highest authorities in the early church. Paul sometimes counts himself in their company on the basis of his encounter with Christ on the Damascus road (Eph. 1:1; see also Gal. 1:1; Rom. 1:1).

Prophets. In the early church, these folk traveled from church to church. They earned no salaries, and because of their itinerant lifestyle they had no families or permanent homes. According to 1 Corinthians 14:3–4, their task was to "speak to other people for their upbuilding and encouragement and consolation."

Evangelists. This term likely refers to missionaries who planted churches. Then, as now, the primary function of evangelists was to bring people into the faith by spreading the good news.

Pastors and teachers. It is not clear whether Paul is describing one office or two here, but most scholars think the phrase represents one group that embodied both aspects in a single ministry. These people worked within a single congregation, where they had the dual responsibility of passing on the gospel to new converts and helping other members grow in the faith.

leaders is to "equip the saints for the work of ministry." In other words, they are charged with the task of empowering all laity so that, together, the work of ministry can be done. The writer knew that one of the ways that God gives us competence is through the gifts with which we are born. Like a gifted singer or artist, we hone and develop our innate skills and abilities through use and practice. We also achieve our greatest potential by working with an accomplished mentor or trainer who can teach us the finer points of our craft. Thus, the writer identified offices in the church designed to give all members the special help they need to develop and use their gifts to the fullest. These leaders are part of God's plan for growing our competency to serve.

A MATTER OF TRUST

It is one thing to read that we are competent in God's service; it is another thing to believe it. Most of us are all too aware of our own shortcomings, and we feel less than competent to serve as an elder or deacon, participate as a worship leader, teach a class, lead a youth group, organize a mission trip, or do any one of the countless other tasks in the church. Nevertheless, Paul assures us that we are competent to do whatever God asks of us. This does not mean we are suited for every task the church has, but it does challenge us to look for those places in the church's ministry where we can contribute.

The problem lies not in our lack of gifts, but in our lack of trust. In that, we can take a lesson from the Hebrew people. After God brought them out of Egypt, they thought the hard part was over. They were soon to learn, however, that they faced a greater challenge than Pharaoh and his army: Now they faced the challenge of trusting God to guide them and provide for them during years in the wilderness.

Such trust did not come easily, when it came at all. Almost from the beginning, for example, the people worried about starvation, and they complained loudly at the prospect.

Despite the people's doubts and fears, God provided food for them. The sustenance came in two forms: (1) a special breadlike substance called manna, and (2) flocks of quail. At least three aspects of this phenomenon have bearing for us in the matter of trusting God to provide nourishment for the community of faith in the form of spiritual gifts:

1. *The provision came in unexpected ways.* The gift of manna was a miracle. Surely the people did not expect this "bread from heaven." Moreover, they were no doubt surprised to find an abundance of quail in the desert as well (Exod. 16).
2. *The provision came when needed.* It did not start on the first day, but on the first day that there was a need.
3. *The provision was sufficient to meet the need at hand.* Those

who followed God's directions about gathering manna always had enough to eat.

In light of all that God did for the Hebrew people, it may be easy for us to look back in hindsight and judge their insecurity harshly. Yet few of us might have done any better. Certainly when it comes to trusting God to give us competence, we tend to falter! This passage reminds us to keep a proper perspective: one of trust.

OUR REASSURANCE

If we have any doubt that God can work through us as we are—or if we want to believe that our current state somehow excuses us from service—we have only to consider John 21:15–19. This passage requires some unpacking of the original language to understand. The scene takes place after the resurrection, when Jesus came to meet some of the disciples on the lakeshore. Poor Peter had been trying to make up with Jesus after denying him three times, and Jesus is about to give him a new assignment.

Before turning to the text we should note, however, that it uses two different verbs for love. The first is *agapao*, from which we get agape, or divine love. The second is *phileo*. This means friendship, or love for one another based on a mutual liking and trust. We see the root of this word today, for example, in "philanthropist," which means one who loves humanity.

In John's account, Jesus uses one word for the most part, and Peter uses the other. Watch for how this affected their exchange.

Jesus began by asking Peter, in essence, "Do you love me with divine love more than these?" Peter responded, "Yes, Lord; you know that I love you as my best and dearest friend." (In other words, Jesus used the word *agapao*, and Peter responded with the word *phileo*.) A second time Jesus asked, "Simon son of John, do you love me with the divine love with which I love you?" Simon Peter answered a second time, "Yes, Lord; you know that I love you as my best and dearest friend." Jesus said to him a third time, "Simon son of John, do you love me as your best and dearest friend?" Peter felt hurt because the third time Jesus used the word *phileo*.

Jesus changed his language to meet Simon Peter where he was. In that moment, Peter saw something in himself he would rather not have seen. Jesus made the invitation twice, "Come up to my level; love me the way I love you." Each time, Peter could only respond as he was capable and say, "Here's where I am." So the third time Jesus said, "OK, I'll be there with you." Personally, I think Peter's hurt was not disappointment in Jesus, but disappointment in himself. He realized what Jesus had done, and he realized his own limitation.

Yet, despite the fact that Peter was not living up to the full promise Jesus saw in him, Jesus did not hesitate to repeat the call to "Feed my sheep." Jesus knew the limits of Simon Peter, and yet he continued to enlist his service. Implicit in the command to "Feed my sheep" is the promise that Peter's gifts will be sufficient to the task at hand.

If we look at the Bible as a whole, in fact, we can find five points of reassurance when we are led to question our competence in God's service.

1. *We don't have to be perfect for God to use our gifts.* Time and again, the Bible shows us God working through imperfect people like Simon Peter. Consider Abraham, for example. In Bible studies and sermons we talk about how God came to Abraham and sent him off into an unknown land and an unknown future. We talk about how Abraham then packed up all his stuff and went, with no hesitation or debate. We don't often discuss, however, the way Abraham soon asked Sarah to pretend to be his sister and marry someone else so that he could sidestep a potentially dangerous situation. Then there's

Jacob, whom the Bible depicts as a master trickster and manip-
ulator. Joseph and his brothers are a model for dysfunctional
family systems. Moses did his best to talk God out of sending
him to Pharaoh and, when God persisted in the call, his final
response amounted to, "Fine, I'll go—but I don't have to like
it!" If God can work through these people, surely God can
work through us.

2. *The divine goal is achievable.* Read the story of the early
church in Acts. Look especially at chapter 4's description of the
early Christian community and the way they shared everything,
including leadership, fellowship, and property. For a little while,
they were the covenant community as God intends it to be. The
ideal did not last, but it existed long enough to show us that the
power to live out God's realm, the power to be competent, is
real and available to us.

3. *God will not let our imperfec-*
tions interfere with reaching the
divine goal. God will keep working through us to accomplish
the goals that God has. Romans
8:28 captures this sense when it
says, "We know that all things
work together for good for those
who love God, who are called
according to his purpose." As
long as we are sincerely seeking
to serve God—and sometimes
even when we are not!—God
will work through us to achieve
divine purposes.

4. *We do each have gifts, and*
the community needs them all.

> ### Ephesians 1:17–19
>
> "I pray that the God of our
> Lord Jesus Christ, the Father of
> glory, may give you a spirit of
> wisdom and revelation as you
> come to know him, so that,
> with the eyes of your heart
> enlightened, you may know
> what is the hope to which he
> has called you, what are the
> riches of his glorious inheri-
> tance among the saints, and
> what is the immeasurable
> greatness of his power for us
> who believe, according to the
> working of his great power."

The affirmation that all are gifted has significant implications
for the church and for how individual members perceive their
roles within Christ's body. It serves as a challenge to each of us

to seek God's gifts in ourselves and others, and it holds us all accountable for bringing those gifts to bear in God's service. We have no excuse on this front. God has given us gifts for the church, and God expects us to use them.

5. *It is in the whole community that we find all the gifts we need, not just in any one person.* Each of us stands in the midst of a community of people who are brothers and sisters, our family in Christ, who are also gifted in some way. Together as a whole we bring competency to our congregations. This is part of God's *sufficiency* at work again. God tells us, in essence, "Only do what you can and that's enough—because if everyone does what he or she can, it will be more than enough." The evidence of this is in the ministries of the church itself, which we will explore in the next chapter.

<hr/>

QUESTIONS FOR REFLECTION

1. What stories from the Bible help you feel competent as a Christian?

2. What do you believe to be the gifts God has given you for service to the church? How did you discover them?

3. Who helped you develop your skills and use them better? How did this happen?

4. In what way does your congregation currently help its members see their gifts and practice them? What more might be done?

KEY LEARNINGS

- As Christians, we are called to use our gifts and talents in the service of the church.

- We are to seek ways to develop and use our gifts to the fullest, and we are to help others do the same.
- We need to trust that we do each have gifts, that the community needs them all, and that they will be sufficient for the tasks at hand.
- It is in the community as a whole that we find all the gifts we need, not just in any one person.

7

Called to Ministry

Ministry, whether that of clergy or laity, begins with calling. In fact, one of the earliest names for the Christian church came from a Greek word whose root meaning is "call." From the beginning, Christians were understood to be those who are "called out" to follow Christ. The response to that call shows in our way of life, including the way we use our gifts to support the church's ministries.

GOD'S HOLY DWELLING PLACE

Being "called out" is intimately related to the biblical concept *holiness*. In both Greek and Hebrew, being "holy" means to be set apart for special use. In our case, we are set apart (or consecrated) as the body of Christ to be a designated place where God's presence comes into the world.

John 1:14 says that in Jesus, "The Word became flesh and

> ### Ephesians 2:10
>
> "For we are what he has made us, created in Christ Jesus for good works, which God prepared beforehand to be our way of life."

lived among us." The Greek word translated "lived" here is literally "tabernacled." In the same way that God's glory and presence filled the tabernacle in the wilderness, making that tent the place where God truly dwelt among the people, so God was present in Jesus Christ. Later, John also describes Jesus' body as being the real temple in which God was present with the people after the wilderness experience ended (John 2:21).

We also are God's temple, both as individuals (1 Cor. 6:19) and as a community (2 Cor. 6:16). Through our union with Christ, the writer of Ephesians says, "the whole structure is joined together and grows into a holy temple in the Lord; in whom you also are built together spiritually into a dwelling place for God" (Eph. 2:21–22). What's more, we are "built upon the foundation of the apostles and prophets, with Christ Jesus himself as the cornerstone" (Eph. 2:20). Christ is the one who holds the whole building together and makes it grow into a sacred temple dedicated to the Lord.

> **Ephesians 2:21–22**
>
> "In him the whole structure is joined together and grows into a holy temple in the Lord; in whom you also are built together spiritually into a dwelling place for God."

A PRIESTHOOD OF ALL BELIEVERS

Using the same temple imagery for the community of faith, the letter of 1 Peter refers to us as "living stones" that are to be "built into a spiritual house" (2:5). This same verse then says we are to be "a holy priesthood." The connection between the two images anticipates the upcoming verse 9, which even more clearly connects our calling as God's people to our purpose in the world: "But you are a chosen race, a royal priesthood, a holy nation, God's own people, *in order that* you may proclaim the mighty acts of him who called you out of darkness into his marvelous light" (italics added). So, we are not just called to be holy; we are also called to be ministers.

Ephesians 4:1–16 also underscores our mutual call to ministry. Even those who are ordained to specific tasks still serve the primary purpose of equipping *all* the saints (that is, the members of Christ's body) "for the work of ministry" (v. 12). The reason each of us has been given the gifts we have is so we can carry out this work of ministry, whatever that may be.

This idea of shared ministry is a central piece of our Reformed theological heritage. One of Martin Luther's great doctrines was that of "the priesthood of all believers," or the idea that each of us is to be a priest to the other. Modern Protestants build on this same belief when we talk about "the ministry of the laity."

Some people still have difficulty speaking about the laity's call to ministry, however, because the word "minister" has come to be associated with minister of the Word and Sacrament. We think of it in terms of someone who is ordained, someone who is set apart for a particular and somewhat narrow set of tasks. That is never the way the word was intended in its usage in the early church years. It was always understood that being in ministry involves the entire covenant community, because of the nature of ministry in a holistic sense.

It may help to recall that, at its heart, the word "minister" refers to someone who administers something. More specifically, the word originally referred to someone who worked in an administrative system to organize order out of chaos and to achieve efficiency through care and oversight. Later this role came to be related to the idea of being a steward. Just as a steward has oversight and care of something, so does a minister. In the church, ministry is having care and oversight of the grace that God has given to us—and that task belongs to us all.

The Bible teaches that we are called and chosen *to service*. God established the covenant community not to give us some kind of special status that exempts us from work, but for the exact opposite. We are set apart for the special purpose of being God's hands in the world. Any time we turn our back on that, we are not living out covenant and we are not participating in the divine vision for bringing about the realm of God on earth.

FOUR TYPES OF MINISTRY WE DO

There are many kinds of ministries we could talk about, but there are four I would like to highlight. These categories are not meant to be definitive, but I find them to be a helpful way of thinking about the different tasks to which we are called.

1. *First is the ministry of care and compassion.* By this I mean a ministry that has its roots in the Old Testament prophets and their call to justice. Like the concept of *shalom*, caring and compassion in the Old Testament always carry a communal sense of justice. When the prophets cry out about the way the poor are cheated, when they cry out about the way orphans and widows are not being cared for, when they cry out about every kind of injustice they see on the streets of their cities, they are standing on the prophetic side of a ministry of care and compassion.

Part of what this ministry involves is being attuned enough to see the people we don't like to see and paying attention to the situations in life and society that we would rather ignore. As Christians we are called to open our eyes to the reality of these situations and to do something about them.

2. *Second is the ministry of comfort.* The ministry of caring and compassion and the ministry of comfort sound very similar, but each serves a different function. The ministry of caring and compassion calls us to be aware of situations in the world, such as hunger and homelessness, that are counter to God's

shalom and to respond accordingly. It is primarily the ministry of social justice.

The ministry of comfort grows out of the Latin roots of that word. *Com* (with) + *fortis* (strength) points us to sharing strength with one another. This kind of comforting is not achieved by putting an arm around someone in pain, patting them on the shoulder, and saying, "Now, now; there, there; it will be OK." Rather, the Christian ministry of comfort involves actively sharing oneself and one's own strength with those who need it.

The apostle Paul often linked prayer with sharing strength. In addition to our physical presence, prayer is one of the primary ways we share strength with one another. Whether it is done from a distance, or sitting side by side, prayer works. It keeps us connected to God and one another.

> **Ephesians 6:18**
>
> "Pray in the Spirit at all times in every prayer and supplication. To that end keep alert and always persevere in supplication for all the saints."

Finally, the ministry of comfort is something that we exchange back and forth. Think about the times in your life that you have really needed to lean on someone and that someone was there. If you are lucky, there was also a time when you were able to return the favor and be there for that person. That is the ministry of comfort to which we are called.

3. *Third is the ministry of confrontation.* We usually don't like this one, but it exists. For a textual reference, see any of the Old Testament prophets and most of Paul's letters! Those who have been through family interventions know they are no fun, but they are sometimes necessary. Likewise, in our Christian family, love should keep us from allowing destructive behavior to continue. Like it or not, if someone's behavior is destructive to self, to others, or to the community, our calling as Christians is to speak out against it in love.

4. *Finally, we are also called to the ministry of construction.* As discussed earlier, our task is to equip the saints for the work of ministry, for building up the body of Christ. In this ministry, each of us is charged with equipping others—especially future generations—to carry on the work of the church. We build up the body so that it can not only survive, but thrive in the years to come.

THE TWELVE STEPS OF PREPARING FOR MINISTRY

The writer of Ephesians makes clear that ministries such as those described above are the responsibility of the Christian community as a whole. We are all to listen to the community of faith and to the promptings of our own hearts to discern which gifts for ministry we have, and then we are to acknowledge, hone, and use those gifts.

All Are Ministers

"Only a few may be called to stand behind a pulpit or baptismal font or communion table. But the task and privilege of the ministry of reconciliation is given to all, clergy and laity alike. To believe in an 'apostolic' church is to believe that every Christian is called and sent out to be a minister, missionary, and servant of God—not just part-time but full-time, whatever his or her occupation. That means you!"
— Guthrie, 365

Yet, when it comes to actually talking about how we prepare for ministry, the answer does not lie in higher education or on-the-job training. Rather, the writer of Ephesians suggests that we become effective for ministry by first preparing ourselves as Christians. This is the point behind Ephesians 6:10–20 and its imagery of soldiers preparing for battle.

A close look at this passage shows twelve things we need to do for our own Christian life. If we follow these instructions, the text implies, we not only can be ready for the tasks of ministry, we can handle all the evils of the world!

1. *"Be strong in the Lord and in the strength of his power"* (v. 10). As we discussed in the previous chapter, our competence for ministry comes from God. The writer of Ephesians says that we do not have to worry about finding the strength and ability in ourselves: God is the source of our power to serve, and God will provide empowerment when the time is right.

2. *"Put on the whole armor of God so that you may be able to . . . stand firm"* (vv. 11–13). In the Bible, "stand firm" almost always carries the sense of standing firm in the faith. For the writer of Ephesians, the concern is partly for our ability to stand against evil (see 6:12) and partly for our ability to hold on to the core of our faith as expressed in 4:4–6. As Ephesians 4:14 says, "We must no longer be children, tossed to and fro and blown about by every wind of doctrine, by people's trickery, by their craftiness in deceitful scheming." Certainly our efforts in ministry should be consistent in reflecting what we believe, and what we believe should "stand firm" within the traditions of the church.

3. *"Stand therefore, and fasten the belt of truth around your waist"* (v. 14a). In a narrow sense, "truth" refers to correct doctrine. Within the overall letter of Ephesians, however, it also refers to the larger truth of God's plan as it is being worked out in the world. Keep sight of that big picture, the writer is saying, and you will know what to do in ministry.

4. *"Put on the breastplate of righteousness"* (v. 14b). In both the Old and New Testaments, "righteousness" refers to ethical and moral behavior in line with God's expectations. As an aspect of our covenant relationship with God and our new life in Christ, righteousness is also an attitude that marks transformed hearts. As such, it naturally extends into our actions and shapes the form our ministry takes.

5. *"As shoes for your feet put on whatever will make you ready to proclaim the gospel of peace"* (v. 15). In the mind of the writer of

Ephesians, the point of the gospel is reconciliation among humans and between humans and God. This is the good news we are to declare in word and deed. Moreover, this goal has deep roots in the Bible's overall understanding of our call to bring God's *shalom* into the world, which lies at the heart of ministry.

6. *"With all of these, take the shield of faith"* (v. 16). In this case, "faith" refers both to the doctrine of the one, true faith as the writer of Ephesians defines it and to our personal relationship with Jesus Christ. Our call to ministry grows out of both, but particularly the latter—it is our response to Jesus' command *to us* to "Feed my sheep."

7. *"Take the helmet of salvation"* (v. 17a). The salvation mentioned here is available to us because of our status as children of God who have been redeemed. It is a condition to which we bear witness in the nature of our Christian life, and our participation in ministry is done in grateful response to it.

8. *"[Also take] the sword of the Spirit, which is the word of God"* (v. 17b). Here we see the one offensive weapon included among the defensive items on this list—Scripture. In the Bible, which the Holy Spirit opens and makes meaningful to us, we find all the necessary clues to see the types of ministry to which God calls us and the purpose they are to achieve.

9. *"Pray in the Spirit at all times . . . in supplication for all the saints"* (v. 18). As we discussed above, prayer is a key element in ministry. It keeps us in touch with God, in communion with Christ, and open to the power of the Spirit. All ministry needs to take place within the context of prayer if it is to be truly effective.

10. *"Pray also for me"* (v. 19a). When the writer of Ephesians asks for the prayers of others, it serves as a challenge to us to do the same. The prayerful support of the community of faith provides a strong and solid base for our ministry efforts.

11. *"[Pray] that when I speak, a message may be given to me to make known with boldness the mystery of the gospel"* (v. 19b). The

writer's next plea builds on the previous one and makes it more specific. The author of Ephesians specifically requests prayers for insight into God's word and for the boldness to proclaim it. This verse stands out as a reminder to us that our number one task in ministry—the purpose that underlies everything else we do—is the proclamation of the gospel.

12. *"I am an ambassador in chains"* (v. 20). It seems that the author of Ephesians was in prison when this letter was written. Nevertheless, those harsh life circumstances do not change the writer's key sense of identity and purpose: "I am an ambassador [for Christ]." In chains or out, we represent our Lord in everything we do, and never more so than when we are performing acts of ministry in his name.

If we were to take all twelve of these statements and condense them into a simple poster showing "Twelve Steps of Preparing for Ministry," it might read something like this:

1. Trust God.
2. Stand firm in the faith.
3. Keep the big picture in mind.
4. Love God with all your heart, mind, soul, and strength, and love your neighbor as yourself.
5. Work for God's *shalom* in all things.
6. Keep your relationship with Jesus healthy and strong.
7. Live as children of God.
8. Study the Bible.
9. Pray for others.
10. Ask others to pray for you.
11. Proclaim the gospel.
12. Be Christ in the world.

A REASON TO HOPE

In Paul's last point above, our calling comes back to the empowerment we receive from the Holy Spirit. This is the same Spirit that Ephesians 1:14 assures us we have received as a *guarantee* or *pledge* that God's purpose is being worked out through us. The presence of the Holy Spirit serves as a "seal" (v. 13) of the promises God has given us, and it gives a reason to maintain our confident hope that those promises will come to fruition. Even more, our experience of the Spirit gives us a foretaste of the future God plans for the whole world.

In addition to the Holy Spirit, we have another assurance that God's purpose really is at work in our lives and in the world: the testimony that God

> raised [Christ] from the dead and seated him at his right hand in the heavenly places, far above all rule and authority and power and dominion, and above every name that is named, not only in this age but also in the age to come. And he has put all things under his feet and has made him the head over all things for the church, which is his body, the fullness of him who fills all in all. (Eph. 1:20–23)

If the story of the good creation was not enough to let us see God's ultimate plan, then this should correct any confusion. In the events of Easter morning, God showed the world an unmistakable blueprint for the future. Christ has been raised from the dead and placed over all creation to ensure that we will truly inherit the fullness of God's promises. All our ministry takes place in this context of waiting for that day to arrive.

⋙⋘⋙⋘⋙

QUESTIONS FOR REFLECTION

1. Where do you see evidence of God's dwelling among the members of your congregation?

2. What ministries exist in your church? Which are performed by pastors? elders and deacons? other lay leaders? you?

3. What do your answers to the above question suggest about how your congregation views "the ministry of the laity"? What are your own views on the idea?

4. What might your congregation do to help all members understand, accept, and be supported in their ministry?

5. What other "Steps in Preparing for Ministry" might you add to the twelve listed above?

KEY LEARNINGS

- We become effective for ministry by first preparing ourselves adequately as Christians.
- As Christians, we are all called to ministry. We have been "set apart" from the rest of the world for service to God, each other, and the world.
- As the body of Christ, the church is the new tabernacle, the place where God dwells in the world.
- There are many ministries within the church, but only one main goal: to bring about a bit of the realm of God into the here and now.

Conclusion

When I met my husband, he had experienced two faith traditions—one as he was growing up and one as a seeker in high school and college. In both he was taught the same thing: that God is a God of judgment and condemnation. This bothered him a great deal because he was also taught that God had, at one point, created laws that human beings could not possibly fulfill, and made them part of a covenant whereby we would always fail. Thus, God appeared to him to have set up humanity in a no-win situation, for no apparent reason. My husband eventually decided the only two logical explanations were that God must either have a warped sense of humor or be a sadistic monster who received pleasure from our condemnation. After telling me this bit of history about himself, he ended by saying, "I just don't want to believe in a God like that." I don't either.

Because my husband thought his two experiences were normative for all Christians, he came to equate being Christian with accepting a God who is either crazy or cruel. Since neither of those was a viable option for him, he eventually ceased thinking of himself as a Christian. In time, however, he was exposed to other versions of Christianity, and his perspective shifted. He realized that he had been taught only bits and pieces of God's story before, and yet those bits and pieces had become the entire lens through which he viewed everything else. So he opted to swap that lens for another. Now when he reads the Bible, he sees grace, redemption, and love instead of judgment, failure, and condemnation. He sees a God who is compassionate, steadfast, and worth loving. He sees a God he likes.

My husband's story is important to me, not just because of my relationship with him, but because of how concretely it shows the matter of perspective. Whether we see the creation story as being primarily about God's goodness or humanity's failure, for example, depends on our perspective. Whether we see the book of Revelation as being primarily about the fullness of the new creation or destruction of those who are left behind also depends on our perspective. This book, start to finish, comes from *my* perspective. That doesn't make its insights necessarily right or wrong; the best I can promise is that they are sincere.

From my perspective, from start to finish the Bible says that our greatest desire as human beings is a world where everything is right—a world where we are in harmony with one another, with our environment, and with our God. Certainly I believe that is God's wish for us and that, from the beginning, God intended us for wholeness as individuals, as a community of faith, and as a world. It was true in Eden, true in the life of biblical Israel, true with Jesus, true in the early church, and it is true now.

Moreover, God has tried all along to show us how to achieve this wholeness. The best way we see this, of course, is in Jesus. In him we have a picture of God incarnate, but we also get a glimpse of the realm of God. Yes, the Bible speaks about failure. Yes, it speaks time and again about the ways we fail to understand, accept, or participate in God's vision for us. Far more, however, it speaks of how God does not give up on us. It is the story of how, *despite us*, God keeps striving for this perfect world on earth. Most of all, it is the story of how God will one day bring creation to this perfect state, no matter what derailments we may throw at the process in the meantime.

The Bible also tells us that God's new creation has, in a sense, already begun in Christ. Because we participate as members of Christ's body in his death and resurrection, new life is available to us now, rather than later. As Marjorie Thompson puts it:

> I believe that life in Christ is a reality already given to us. It is ours to claim if we have the courage to enter it. And it really is new. Life in Christ is different from the patterns of the world we know so well. In place of degradation and abuse, it means reverence and respect for all of life. Instead of the politics of power, it embodies humble and joyful service. In place of retribution and revenge, it offers forgiveness and reconciliation. Beyond the forces of disease and death, it holds out healing and life. Instead of fear and anxiety, it offers trust in God. Life in the Spirit means release from idols and freedom from addictions. Christ provides realistic hope for a realistic life. He is the wellspring for our thirst, the bread for every hunger of the human heart. "O taste and see that the LORD is good!" (Ps. 34:8). Once we have tasted living bread and drunk living water, we will be able to lead others who hunger and thirst to our common vital Source.[1]

Within our new life in Christ, we have a place where we belong (the church) and we have an identity (children of God). What's more, both *place* and *identity* stretch out through eternity. The roots of this community to which we belong and the roots of who we are literally begin at creation, and they have their ultimate ending point in that glorious time when, someday, God makes all things right again.

We live in this in-between tension, in which God's realm has begun to come on earth in a new and radically different way in the incarnation of Christ, but isn't here in fullness yet, and everything we do as Christians is shaped by it. We remember the biblical stories because they help us understand where we come from and who we are; we anticipate the glories God has promised because they tell us where we are headed and who we are intended to be; and in both we find the measure of our Christian hope and responsibility. In the meantime, we work at claiming and maintaining our sense of place and identity in the present time, as we strive to embody God's vision in all that we say and do.

> Now to him who by the power at work within us is able to accomplish abundantly far more than all we can ask or imagine, to him be glory in the church and in Christ Jesus to all generations, forever and ever. Amen. (Eph. 3:20–21)

Appendix A

Background on Covenant

This section provides additional insights into the three examples of human-to-human covenants described in chapter 2. Leaders using this book in a small group study will find this background information helpful in preparing the session(s) on covenant.

DAVID AND JONATHAN

First Samuel 18:1–4 says of Jonathan and David:

> When David had finished speaking to Saul, the soul of Jonathan was bound to the soul of David, and Jonathan loved him as his own soul. Saul took him that day and would not let him return to his father's house. Then Jonathan made a covenant with David, because he loved him as his own soul. Jonathan stripped himself of the robe that he was wearing, and gave it to David, and his armor, and even his sword and his bow and his belt.

The covenant between David and Jonathan was an expression of their incredible friendship with each other, and it was soon

to be tested by an intensely complicated situation. The rest of
1 Samuel 18 shows that Jonathan's father, King Saul, was
becoming somewhat emotionally unbalanced. Jealous of
David's military successes and public popularity, he began to
see the younger man as a threat to his own position.

Despite some of David's previous exploits, the biblical
writer goes to lengths to show that he was a loyal subject and
that Saul's emotions were out of control. Not long after the
covenant takes place, we find Saul looking for David to kill
him. Jonathan was stuck in the unenviable position of having
to make a choice between his father, whom he loved, and his
dearest friend, whom he also loved. First Samuel 20 makes it
clear that Jonathan's subsequent loyalty to David was rooted
in their covenant relationship.

Note that the covenant account mentions an exchange of
clothes between the two men: "Jonathan made a covenant with
David, because he loved him as his own soul. Jonathan
stripped himself of the robe that he was wearing, and gave it
to David, and his armor, and even his sword and his bow and
his belt" (vv. 3–4). The robe was probably the symbol of
Jonathan's status as the heir apparent, which he passed off to
David. Giving over the armor and weapons was the action of
a vassal swearing allegiance to a lord. All of this points to
Jonathan's allegiance to David, not just as beloved friend, but
as the king who was to be.

So the covenant that Jonathan made with David had ramifications on two levels. On a purely personal level, it was a way
of saying to David, "I will stick by you no matter what—I will
not choose my father over you." The covenant also extended
into the political sphere, however, because Jonathan was, in
essence, saying, "When the time comes, I will support you
over my father." As the eldest son of Saul, he was even saying,
"I abdicate my right to rule in order to establish your right to
rule."

Despite the tricky political situation, however, the heart of the covenant still resides in that key phrase: "because he loved him as his own soul." Note that not only is this a covenant between two individuals, but it is meant to give a voluntary and sacred stamp to feelings that are already there. Because their friendship ran so deep, Jonathan and David wanted to give it formality. They wanted to establish it in the sight of God.

Given that texts outside the Bible describe similar covenant ceremonies, it seems reasonable to conclude that this single instance in the Bible reflects an established experience in the society of the day. In other words, this type of covenant between friends is not something that Jonathan and David invented; they would have known of the practice from their own culture. Granted, such covenants were rare, in that people reserved them for celebrating only the strongest of friendships, but they were not unknown. These covenants were understood to be a way of indicating friendships that would last to the death.

JACOB AND LABAN

The account of the covenant between Jacob and Laban reads as follows:

> Then Laban answered and said to Jacob, . . . "Come now, let us make a covenant, you and I; and let it be a witness between you and me." So Jacob took a stone, and set it up as a pillar. And Jacob said to his kinsfolk, "Gather stones," and they took stones, and made a heap; and they ate there by the heap. Laban called it Jegar-sahadutha: but Jacob called it Galeed. Laban said, "This heap is a witness between you and me today." Therefore he called it Galeed, and the pillar Mizpah, for he said, "The LORD watch between you and me, when we are absent one from the other. If you ill-treat my daughters, or if you take wives in addition to my daughters, though no one else is with

us, remember that God is witness between you and me."

Then Laban said to Jacob, "See this heap and see the pillar, which I have set between you and me. This heap is a witness, and the pillar is a witness, that I will not pass beyond this heap to you, and you will not pass beyond this heap and this pillar to me, for harm. May the God of Abraham and the God of Nahor"— the God of their father—"judge between us." So Jacob swore by the Fear of his father Isaac, and Jacob offered a sacrifice on the height and called his kinsfolk to eat bread; and they ate bread and tarried all night in the hill country.

Early in the morning Laban rose up, and kissed his grandchildren and his daughters and blessed them; then he departed and returned home. (Gen. 31:43–55)

From this account, we get some clues as to what tribal covenants were like in biblical times and as to why they were needed. There are at least five points in which this covenant seems typical of other such agreements in the ancient Near East:

1. *It is a tribal agreement.* Both whole tribes are involved, not just these two men.

2. *It is based on mutual insecurity.* Unlike David and Jonathan, who loved and trusted each other, Jacob and Laban had a very strained relationship, full of animosity and distrust. They sought peace through a covenant agreement because each sought security from the other. It is as if they said, "The only way we can ease ourselves out of this distrust is to have a relationship that is so binding we think maybe the other won't break it."

3. *It involves a memorial.* Jacob and Laban set up a pillar called "watchtower" to remind themselves of the treaty, but it is also a watchtower for God, in that they call on God to be a witness to the covenant agreement. Notice their parting words: "The LORD watch between you and me, when we are

absent one from the other." Does this sound familiar? Some congregations refer to these words as the Mizpah benediction and use them as a blessing to close worship services. In this case, however, Jacob and Laban were not pronouncing a blessing. They were saying, in essence, "May the Lord watch between you and me, while we are absent one from the other, so that you don't cheat! I don't trust you, but God is watching you, so maybe you'll behave."

4. *Both sides take oaths.* That is common in covenants; both sides must participate in the agreement. The points of compromise are somewhat implicit in the text, but it seems that Laban promises to let Jacob go on his way in peace, without further threat of harm, and Jacob promises not to mistreat his wives, Laban's daughters, out of pique with their father.

5. *The parties share a common meal.* This is a theme that will come back in the covenants with God. It is a theme that continues in the church today: The importance of sitting at the Lord's Table, sharing a common meal with one another, continues to be part of the celebration of the covenant of God.

NATIONAL TREATIES

The historical records of Assyria and Babylon show that treaties between kings followed a set form. Each of these political treaties had six parts. First was the preamble. The preamble just says that one ruler is going to make an agreement with another. Sometimes the preamble in the Bible is as simple as "And then Moses said to the people," but there is always an introduction of some kind that points to the covenant language about to follow.

Next comes a historical prologue. In ancient Near Eastern treaties, this prologue cataloged all the things that each ruler had done for the other. It presented a history of the relationship. We find that in the biblical covenants as well. The covenants with God detail the history of the relationship between God and the community of faith.

The third section provides the stipulations. Those we recognize! The stipulations in God's covenants may be as simple as the Ten Commandments or as complex as the books of Numbers and Leviticus. The stipulations spell out the details of the covenant agreement; they state the terms by which each party agrees to abide.

Then each historical treaty (or covenant) stipulates where the text will be kept and when the text will be brought out for a public reading to the people. Ancient treaty makers understood that terms could be easily forgotten or misremembered without such scheduled memory aids. We find the same thing in the biblical covenants. Provisions are made in the Mosaic covenant (Deut. 31:10–13) and when Joshua reestablished the covenant with the people (Joshua 24) to bring the covenant formally before the people on a regular basis. They understood that if they did not go back to the agreement on a regular basis, then an older generation can forget the terms and a younger one might never learn them. It has to be made new for the people time and time again, and the biblical writers understood how especially true that was for the covenants with God.

Then there is a list of witnesses, often divine ones. For example, in the Assyrian treaties, two rulers sometimes called on four or five local gods to be witnesses to the treaty between them.

The set of witnesses is then followed by a list of blessings and curses. They are always there, stipulating what will happen if one keeps the covenant and what will happen if one does not.

Appendix B

The Blood of the Covenant

This section provides additional insights into the blood imagery associated with covenants in both the Old and New Testaments. Leaders using this book in a small-group study will find this background information helpful in preparing the session(s) on covenant.

THE SINAI EVENT

In Exodus 24:1–8, we find the ritual of covenant ratification that dramatizes the uniting of two parties, God and Israel. We also find the use of sacrificial blood to seal the covenant.

The most common phrase in the Bible for making a covenant literally means "to cut a covenant," because the official ceremony involved cutting an animal to be served as the main dish in a common meal between the parties. This happened at Sinai, as we see in the text:

> Then [God] said to Moses, "Come up to the LORD, you and Aaron, Nadab, and Abihu, and seventy of the

elders of Israel, and worship at a distance. Moses alone shall come near the LORD; but the others shall not come near, and the people shall not come up with him."

Moses came and told the people all the words of the LORD and all the ordinances; and all the people answered with one voice, and said, "All the words that the LORD has spoken we will do." And Moses wrote down all the words of the LORD. He rose early in the morning, and built an altar at the foot of the mountain, and set up twelve pillars, corresponding to the twelve tribes of Israel. He sent young men of the people of Israel, who offered burnt offerings and sacrificed oxen as offerings of well-being to the LORD. Moses took half of the blood and put it in basins, and half of the blood he dashed against the altar. Then he took the book of the covenant, and read it in the hearing of the people; and they said, "All that the LORD has spoken we will do, and we will be obedient." Moses took the blood and dashed it on the people, and said, "See the blood of the covenant that the LORD has made with you in accordance with all these words."

When Moses took some of the blood of the slaughtered animal and sprinkled it on the people, that was part of ratifying the covenant.

In the Hebrew understanding, blood is life, the most sacred thing on earth. Because it brings life to a body, human or otherwise, blood is the one thing on earth most invested with God's own divine presence and spirit. The symbolism of blood is the symbolism of both forgiveness and healing, because it is through blood that God gives us the vitality that is life. Blood is just as powerful a force in the human body (and other creaturely bodies) as is breath, which is also a very sacred term in Hebrew.

So when Moses took the blood and sprinkled it on the congregation, they did not associate this with death; rather, it was a sign of the life that only God can give. It was a sign of entering into the new life that the covenant represented.

If we carry this concept into the New Testament and its use of the phrase "blood of the covenant" (i.e., in Christ), then we can see the sacredness and the life-centeredness of the blood imagery there. Moreover, we can trace the development of the understanding of *blood*, particularly the blood of Christ, through each of the Gospels.

The oldest Gospel, Mark, has Jesus saying at the Last Supper, "This is my blood of the covenant, which is poured out for many" (Mark 14:24). Although some ancient manuscripts read "blood of the *new* covenant," the most reliable ones do not have this phrase. Matthew puts the same words in Jesus' mouth—"This is my blood of the covenant, which is poured out for many"—but adds "for the forgiveness of sins" (Matt. 26:28). By the time we get to Luke, the phrase reads "This cup that is poured out for you is the new covenant in my blood" (Luke 22:20).

Clearly, some theological interpretation has taken place along the way. By Luke's day, the cup at the supper was no longer representative of the covenant that the Hebrew people (and the early Jewish Christians) claimed for themselves. "The covenant" has become something else, something much more tied to the new work that God did in Christ. In addition, notice that the phrase moves from "poured out for many" (Mark 14:24; Matt. 26:28) to "poured out for you" (Luke 22:20). There is a decided shift in focus when it comes to the perceived beneficiaries of the shedding of Jesus' life-giving blood.

Appendix C

Pronunciation Guide for Greek, Hebrew, and Latin Words

Adamah	ad-ah-mah'
Adoptio	ad-op'-tee-oh
Adrogatio	ad-ro-gah'-tee-oh
Agape	ag-ah'-pay
Agapao	ag-ap-ah'-o
Aretz	eh'-rets
Berith	ber-eeth'
Diatheke	dee-ath-ay'-kay
Hesed	keh'-sed
Mesites	mess-ee'-tace
Phileo	phil'-ay-oh
Shalom	shah-loam'
Shema	shuh-mah'
Teleo	tel-eh'-o

Notes

Introduction

1. Some of the material in this book grew out of preparation for presentations made at the Montreat Christian Education Conference of July 23–28, 2000.

Chapter 1: An Overarching Plan

1. For more on this concept, see Jon D. Levenson, *Creation and the Persistence of Evil* (Princeton, N.J.: Princeton University Press, 1994).
2. M. Eugene Boring, *Revelation*, Interpretation (Louisville, Ky.: Westminster/John Knox, 1989), 222.
3. Ibid., 221–22.
4. Ibid., 224.

Chapter 2: Called to Relationship

1. See, for example, the research presented in Andrew Newberg, *Why God Won't Go Away: Brain Science and the Biology of Belief* (New York: Ballantine Books, 2001).
2. One might also wonder about Ruth and Naomi in this regard. Wasn't their relationship a type of covenant like Jonathan's and David's? The answer is yes and no. On the level of emotional commitment, they certainly model what a covenant relationship is supposed to be. David and Jonathan are unique, however, in that they represent the only case where the word *berith* is used to describe a relationship between two individuals. Moreover,

they represent the only case where two individuals establish a formal relationship of *berith* through a ceremony.

3. The account of this covenant in 1 Sam. 18:1–4 can give the false impression that the relationship was one-way, with Jonathan making all the concessions to David. Subsequent texts indicate this is not the case, though. For example, in 2 Sam. 9, David takes Jonathan's son under his protection, rather than killing him like the other males in the family line. David says at the time, "I will show you kindness for the sake of your father Jonathan" (v. 7), which many take as a reference back to David's own obligations under the covenant made with Jonathan.

4. Josh. 24:22 says that Joshua called on the people at Shechem to be witnesses against themselves in their covenant with God!

5. Marjorie J. Thompson, *SoulFeast* (Louisville, Ky.: Westminster John Knox, 1995), 135–36.

6. Shirley C. Guthrie, *Christian Doctrine*, rev. ed. (Louisville: Westminster John Knox, 1994), 296.

Chapter 4: Called to a New Identity

1. Prov. 17:2 and 19:10 may also refer to this practice.

2. Ralph Martin, *Ephesians, Colossians, and Philemon*, Interpretation (Louisville, Ky.: Westminster/John Knox, 1991), 20.

Chapter 5: Called to a Way of Life

1. Luke 23:45 places this event just before Jesus' death.

2. Martin, *Ephesians, Colossians, and Philemon*, 49.

3. Ibid., 34.

Conclusion

1. Thompson, *SoulFeast*, 16.

For Further Reading

Boring, M. Eugene. *Revelation*. Interpretation. Louisville, Ky.: Westminster/John Knox, 1989.

Donelson, Lewis R. *Colossians, Ephesians, First and Second Timothy, and Titus*. Westminster Bible Companion. Louisville, Ky.: Westminster John Knox, 1996.

Dykstra, Craig. *Growing in the Life of Faith*. Louisville, Ky.: Westminster John Knox, 1999.

Guthrie, Shirley C. *Christian Doctrine*. Rev. ed. Louisville, Ky.: Westminster John Knox, 1994.

Levenson, Jon D. *Creation and the Persistence of Evil*. Princeton, N.J.: Princeton University Press, 1994.

Martin, Ralph. *Ephesians, Colossians, and Philemon*. Interpretation. Louisville, Ky.: Westminster/John Knox, 1991.

Newberg, Andrew. *Why God Won't Go Away: Brain Science and the Biology of Belief*. New York: Ballantine Books, 2001.

Rhodes, Arnold B. *The Mighty Acts of God*. Rev. ed. By W. Eugene March. Louisville, Ky.: Geneva Press, 2000.

Thompson, Marjorie J. *SoulFeast*. Louisville, Ky.: Westminster John Knox, 1995.